ANTONIO

DO YOU BELIEVE?

Antonio Monda teaches in the Kanbar Institute of Film and Television, Tisch School of the Arts, at New York University. He has curated exhibitions and retrospectives for the Museum of Modern Art, the Guggenheim Museum, the Film Society of Lincoln Center, the National Gallery in Washington, and the Rome Auditorium. He is an award-winning filmmaker, the cofounder and artistic director of the literary festival Le Conversazioni, the author of *La magnifica illusione* (*A Journey into American Cinema,* 2003), and, with Mary Lea Bandy, the editor of *The Hidden God* (2004). He writes for *La Repubblica* and is the film critic for *La Rivista dei Libri.*

Ann Goldstein has translated works by, among others, Primo Levi, Pier Paolo Pasolini, Alessandro Baricco, Elena Ferrante, and Roberto Calasso. She has been a recipient of the PEN Renato Poggioli Award, a grant from the National Italian American Foundation, and a translation award from the Italian Ministry of Foreign Affairs.

DO YOU BELIEVE

DO YOU BELIEVE

?

CONVERSATIONS ON GOD AND RELIGION

Antonio Monda

TRANSLATED FROM THE ITALIAN BY ANN GOLDSTEIN

VINTAGE BOOKS
A Division of Random House, Inc.
New York

A VINTAGE BOOKS ORIGINAL, NOVEMBER 2007

Translation copyright © 2007 by Fazi Editore

All rights reserved. Published in the United States by Vintage Books,
a division of Random House, Inc., New York, and in Canada by
Random House of Canada Limited, Toronto. Originally published in
Italy as *Tu credi?* by Fazi Editore srl, Rome, in 2006.
Copyright © 2006 by Antonio Monda.
Copyright © 2006 by Fazi Editore srl.

Vintage and colophon are registered trademarks of Random House, Inc.

Grateful acknowledgment is made to Farrar, Straus and Giroux, LLC, for
permission to reprint an excerpt from "The Schooner *Flight*" from *Collected Poems
1948–1984* by Derek Walcott, copyright © 1986 by Derek Walcott; and excerpts from
"Pentecost" from *The Arkansas Testament* by Derek Walcott, copyright © 1987 by
Derek Walcott. Reprinted by permission of Farrar, Straus and Giroux, LLC

Library of Congress Cataloging-in-Publication Data
Monda, Antonio.
[Tu credi? English]
Do you believe? : conversations on God and religion / by Antonio Monda ;
translated from the Italian by Ann Goldstein.
p. cm.
ISBN 978-0-307-28058-9 (alk. paper)
1. United States—Religion—1960–.   2. Interviews—United States.   I. Title.
BL2525.M6513 2007
200.92'273—dc22
2007014749

Book design by Jo Anne Metsch

www.vintagebooks.com

Printed in the United States of America
10 9 8 7 6 5 4 3 2 1

To Jacquie,
who saves me every day

———————

The idea of God as an omniscient, omnipotent being, who moreover loves us, is one of the most daring creations of fantastic literature. All the same, I would prefer that the idea of God belonged to realistic literature.

—Jorge Luis Borges

CONTENTS

xi

Contents

DO YOU BELIEVE

The Evidence of Things Unseen

Faith is the substance of things hoped for, the evidence
of things unseen.

St. Paul, Letter to the Hebrews, 11:1

When I decided to undertake these dialogues with
well-known American cultural figures about their
relationship with the existence of God, I was well aware that
it was a journey with deeply personal implications. It's a
journey that holds more questions than answers, unless one
accepts the logic of faith—an expression that for those who
are not believers is, in essence, an oxymoron.

During the final months of preparing the manuscript I
was surprised to find friends and colleagues repeatedly asking, "Why did you decide to write a book like this?" In most
cases they asked with great affection and respect; yet the

question itself, and the underlying tone of astonishment, disconcerted me.

What subjects should one write about? I wondered, and then I thought, Is there any subject more urgent?

I am aware, of course, that in this book a universal theme has been limited to the world of American culture, yet the question had to do with the choice of subject, not with the fact that I had decided to limit it to a geographic or cultural area. Numerous books on religion have been published recently, and religion obviously has played a central role in the important and often dramatic political and social choices of recent years. So the astonishment had more to do with the fact that my book was intended not as a sociopolitical analysis but, rather, as an attempt—although perhaps provocative, without, I think it's fair to say, any intellectual subtext—to ask and ask oneself about the heart of the matter. It is an attempt to reclaim religion's central place in existence, with a consistent emphasis on how every choice (existential, artistic, political) has its origins directly and inevitably in the answer given to the great question.

Do You Believe? is constructed around a simple but fundamental question: I asked the people I interviewed to tell me honestly if they think that God exists, and how their answer to this question has affected their choices in life.

I would be lying if I said that people's reactions when

asked if they would be interviewed were immediately enthu-
siastic; in fact, almost all those I approached were puzzled at
first, and asked for time to think about it. Some wanted to
know in advance what questions I would ask and others
wanted to be able to correct their responses before publication. In the end, only a few people declined to participate in
my project, and those who were willing responded with passion and generosity.

In light of my experiences both with those who were
interviewed and with friends and colleagues who followed
the book's progress, I think I can say that the responses I
encountered while I was working on it revealed a range of
attitudes, from the healthy, legitimate modesty of those who
prefer not to discuss such matters in public to a refusal to
confront such matters on the part of those who are com-
fortably set in their convictions. My research and my interviews ultimately persuaded me that the existence of God is
indeed the big question, from which all others derive, but
what seems to me interesting is a tendency—as human, in
my opinion, as it is disquieting—to minimize the implications of the resulting questions, especially in the case of
those who say they believe.

If God exists, how does he speak to us? What does he tell
us? Are we able to understand his language? And how do
we speak to him?

Too often, on both sides of the Atlantic, I have come across people who recognize the existence of God, yet confine his presence to a mystery that in fact leaves one free to behave however one sees fit or, at most, according to the canons of a vague idea of goodness. I also met people who declare that they believe in a particular codified religion but who oppose or challenge some of the norms of that religion. I have problems with this attitude and, from the perspective of my own religion, I've always found less than convincing the position of those who recognize the existence of God and the divinity of Christ but dispute (or even have contempt for) the Church. I certainly don't mean to say that the Church of Rome hasn't made mistakes, even serious ones, in the course of its long history, but I want to emphasize that the believer can't not know that Christ entrusted the keys to Peter, investing with complete authority the disciple who denied him three times during the night before the Crucifixion. In the words of G. K. Chesterton, in his book *Heretics:* "When Christ at a symbolic moment was establishing His great society, He chose for its corner-stone neither the brilliant Paul nor the mystic John, but a shuffler, a snob, a coward—in a word, a man. And upon this rock He has built His Church, and the gates of Hell have not prevailed against it. All the empires and the kingdoms have failed, because of this inherent and continual weakness, that they were founded by strong men and upon strong men. But this one thing, the historic Christian Church, was founded on a weak man, and for that reason it is indestructible. For no chain is stronger than its weakest link."

A conviction like Chesterton's originates in a profound faith (and it's illuminating, to say the least, that this book was written seventeen years before Chesterton's conversion to Catholicism), but I don't think that anyone, even those who consider religion a disaster, a lie, or "the opiate of the people," can help feeling a sense of mystery before the central place still occupied by this two-thousand-year-old institution constructed by weak men who have often cursed and betrayed its message. And the sense of mystery can only conceal a doubt: Is there something truly divine behind it?

Chesterton's insight about the indestructible weak force goes along with the thesis of *L'Impur,* a book by the French writer Jean Guitton about the Catharist heresy, which has Gnostic origins and intersects the history of the Church. Guitton dares to prefer the impure over the pure, with the purpose of saving the true: in the knowledge that purity is the temptation of the man who believes himself an angel— who takes refuge from life lived, with all its compromises, and impatiently wants to separate the weeds from the good seed. To use Guitton's words: "The devil is the image of the angel. Catharism is the temptation of great souls, of elevated consciences, of disinterested beings. It's the analogue of the angelic sin."

The temptation of Catharism seems to me the other side of the New Age spiritual tendencies currently so fashionable. Against an unattainable purity is set a religion constructed for the use of the individual worshipper, with elastic standards that contradict the sense of the etymon *religio:* "bond." Orthodoxy (and obviously I'm not referring just to Catholicism) paradoxically becomes the root of the problem precisely because of the daily abnegation it demands, which prides itself on its *aurea mediocritas,* its golden mean; and it also becomes the enemy to combat or deride on the part of those who have chosen the two extremes of Catharism and the vague New Age cult of the personal. Yet it also becomes, dangerously, the fertile ground in which every type of fundamentalist aberration can proliferate.

I think that beyond the examples of the sublime and the warrior, the fundamental genetic makeup of the believer includes not only the choice of the golden mean but its celebration. As Robert Louis Stevenson writes in "A Christmas Sermon": "We require higher tasks, because we do not recognise the height of those we have. Trying to be kind and honest seems an affair too simple and too inconsequential for gentlemen of our heroic mould; we had rather set ourselves to something bold, arduous, and conclusive; we had rather found a schism or suppress a heresy, cut off a hand or mortify an appetite. But the task before us, which is to co-endure with our existence, is rather one of microscopic fineness, and the heroism required is that of patience. There is no cutting of the Gordian knots of life; each must be smilingly unravelled."

It will be evident by now that the author is a believer (full disclosure: Catholic, Apostolic, Roman), and no one, myself least of all, can escape his own upbringing and his own convictions. In the process of writing this book, however, I tried to maintain a certain detachment, and I think I can say honestly that I learned a lot, especially from those whose convictions are very different from mine, whether they belong to another faith or are atheists or agnostics.

I tried to stay as far as possible from the news and the polemics of recent times, in an attempt to have a dialogue on the essential questions, from which, I would like to say again, every attitude derives. I know I have been indiscreet in many cases, and perhaps also impertinent, but I think I have succeeded in establishing a sincere and, I hope, useful dialogue with a wide variety of people, toward all of whom I feel both gratitude and affection.

Two people whom I had the privilege to know, Susan Sontag and Arthur Miller, died while I was working on the book. I know that they would have made an invaluable contribution and I confess that I feel their absence. I also regret the absence of Muhammad Ali, who declared his interest in participating, but was unable to for reasons of health.

A number of the people interviewed here were not born in America, and in some cases only recently chose it as their home. This is not a limitation but, rather, may help make the book a particularly meaningful reflection of this country. I have lived in America for twelve years and have learned to love it in all its contradictions. But above all I have seen the central place of religion in daily life, in political and artistic choices. A poll published in *Newsweek* in September 2005 revealed a series of facts that seems to me significant: according to research conducted by Beliefnet, using a sample of 1,004 people, 24 percent of Americans define themselves as spiritual but not religious, 9 percent as religious but not spiritual, 55 percent as religious and spiritual, and only 8 percent as neither religious nor spiritual (4 percent answered "I don't know"). It remains to be seen, obviously, how those interviewed define the difference between religious and spiritual, but it seems equally significant that 57 percent of the population attributes a fundamental importance to spirituality in daily life, and that this is true of 44 percent of people under forty. Religion therefore seems present in a fundamental manner even among the young.

According to the poll, 33 percent of the country is evangelical Protestant, 25 percent Protestant but not evangelical,

22 percent Catholic, 1 percent Jewish, 1 percent Muslim. The number of Christians who don't belong to these faiths is 5 percent, while the number of non-Christians is 3 percent. Those who are atheists or agnostics or who do not belong to any religion make up 10 percent.

With respect to the issues that I tried to address in the book, some facts turn out to be particularly interesting. To the question "Why are you observant?" 39 percent answered, "In order to establish a personal relationship with God"; 30 percent, "To become a better person and live ethically"; 17 percent, "To find peace and happiness"; 10 percent, "To be in touch with something greater"; 8 percent, "To give meaning to life"; and 3 percent, "To be part of a community."

Twenty percent of those interviewed in the poll had changed their faith since childhood, but only 4 percent had definitively abandoned religion.

Seventy-nine percent of those interviewed think that a person of another faith can attain salvation, and within this percentage 68 percent of the evangelical Protestants answered affirmatively, 83 percent of the nonevangelical Protestants, 91 percent of the Catholics, and 73 percent of the non-Christians.

Eighty percent of those interviewed think that the universe was created by God, and 67 percent believe that after death the soul will go to Heaven or Hell. (The other percentage is significant: 13 percent deny the existence of

Heaven and Hell, but believe that the soul survives in a spiritual form; 6 percent deny the existence of the soul and identify death with the end of everything; 5 percent believe in reincarnation; and 9 percent "don't know.") To a question about the primary importance of prayer, 27 percent answered that they pray "to seek the guidance of God," 23 percent "to thank him," 19 percent "to be close to him," 13 percent "to help others," 9 percent "to improve themselves." Finally, there are data that allow us to read in a broad manner religious and sentimental relations within the melting pot: 70 percent are married to a person of the same faith; 14 percent to a person of a similar religion; 5 percent to someone of a somewhat different faith; and 10 percent to someone extremely different.

A reflection on faith is inevitably diminished by a collection of numerical data, yet the fact that 90 percent of Americans—or people who live in America—call themselves believers is impressive, especially in contrast to the sample offered in this book (around 40 percent call themselves believers). The number of people I talked to is certainly a modest basis on which to construct a significant sample, but that deficiency has to be weighed against the reputation and cultural importance of the people themselves. And this fact leads to a further, contradictory reflection: should we deduce that the presence of faith and religion fades—or even disappears—when the sample in question is made up of intellectuals, or should we recall the words of St. Matthew when Christ prays to his father, blessing him: "Because thou hast hid these things from the wise and prudent, and hast revealed them unto babes"? It is one of the many points along this journey where the questions are more provocative than the answers.

The poll contains much other interesting information, allowing us to give religious choices a political interpretation as well (from geographic divisions to racial), but what seems to me especially significant, and what guided the reflections that led to this book, is the answer to the key question, preceding every type of political, ideological, and even artistic choice. For example, can an artist who says he is observant create something in which God is absent (or indifferent)? Can an artist who is a believer not feel obligated to bear witness to what he calls faith?

Two years ago, Mary Lea Bandy and I put together an anthology of essays entitled *The Hidden God* to accompany a film retrospective at the Museum of Modern Art. The idea was to analyze a series of films from all over the world in which the idea of divinity, and hence of faith, was hidden. Obviously the films make reference to various types of religious expression, and I was struck by the fact that I could not find any reflection of spirituality in some films that I love deeply. Furthermore, artistic reflection on spirituality is nearly absent in films from the greatest directors—for example, Luchino Visconti. As we were putting together the book and the show, I asked a critic I respect enormously in what films he thought God was present. His answer was "All," but I have to point out that the person in question, in addition to being a critic, is a Jesuit priest. I probably don't have either his faith or his capacity for analysis, but with equal passion I would try to turn his suggestion around and ask how an artist who wishes to live the teaching of the Gospel in his daily life should behave. The discussion could be expanded to include every other choice in life; in fact, it could be applied to every other faith. The events of recent years impose on us this question in particular: What is the line between bearing witness and extremism, between choosing to follow the teachings of a revealed religion and fundamentalism? Personally I feel that having faith allows us the greatest freedom in secular life, precisely because it leads to a genuine and complete detachment from any possible ideological or bigoted attitude. But this conviction cannot escape the fact of human frailty: of material interests and passions, as well as the angelic temptations I mentioned earlier. And so there is bigotry, which can affect both believers and nonbelievers.

And, reflecting on human frailty, one returns to Chesterton's insight about the very institution of the Church, with all its contradictions—which I don't think have impugned, even marginally, the truth of its teaching. In 1965 the theologian Karl Rahner wrote: "The Church would be not the true people of God but a purely ideal reality, of almost mythical character, if one thought that the state of sin of its members determined it." And he concludes: "If one realizes clearly that the earthly Church remains a church of sinners, one understands exactly how and why it is the holy Church."

In dialogues between atheists and believers the idea of respect recurs often: to me this idea seems an observation both obvious and insufficient. The immediate temptation is to consider such an attitude simple hypocrisy (I would find it difficult to feel intellectual respect for a person who believes in something nonexistent to the point of giving it existence), but then one becomes aware that this respect is marked by doubt and by what believers call the mystery of faith. And I can't help but think of the extraordinary assertion of St. Paul in the Letter to the Hebrews: "Faith is the substance of things hoped for, the evidence of things unseen."

For those who believe, the answer lies there, and I was much struck by the fact that it was a nonbeliever, Richard Ford, who urged me to reflect on this passage, confessing that it returns constantly to his thoughts.

This book is certainly in no way exhaustive, but I hope

that it may prove to be a good traveling companion on the most important journey of every life. The outcome is not certain, but on an adventure like this, the Greek philosophers put it best: *Kalos gar o kindynos,* "Risk is beautiful."

—*Antonio Monda, January 2006*

PAUL AUSTER

A Mocking and Unfathomable Mystery

I've known Paul Auster for many years, and I have to admit that for a long time I was sorry that he was so unwilling to talk about his personal relationship with religion. I realize that it's a delicate subject, and that each sensibility experiences it in a different way, and yet I somehow felt that he owed me that sort of confidence. Obviously, I was wrong, but then, especially after September 11, 2001, our relationship gained a certain intimacy, nourished by long conversations about politics (his positions are definitely more radical than mine), about cinema (I admire the humility he has demonstrated as a writer learning about film), and about Brooklyn, where he lives, and which in his latest novel he calls "the ancient kingdom."

Paul is a great storyteller, and his inability to contain his laughter when he is telling a funny story is irresistible. Some of his favorite stories are about Billy Wilder, a director we both love, and among the many anecdotes he recounts, my favorite is one that I think explains his conception of life. Wilder, on the occasion of his ninetieth birthday, was to receive an important prize intended as a tribute to his entire career. All Hollywood had gathered to honor him, and at least three generations of producers, directors, actors, and other film people gave the master a standing ovation as soon as he appeared in the theater. Wilder made his way to the stage with some difficulty, accepted the award, and then headed toward the microphone that had been set up for his thank-you speech. This rhetorical moment has enormous importance in Hollywood, and the excitement in the theater was palpable. Finally reaching the microphone, Wilder began to speak, in his unmistakable Austrian accent: "A man goes to the doctor and says anxiously, 'Doctor, I can't pee anymore!' The doctor, perplexed, looks at the man and asks him, 'How old are you?' And the man says, 'Ninety.' 'Well,' the doctor replies, 'you've peed enough.'" Without another word Wilder put the microphone back in its place and left the stage, leaving the audience in a state of mingled dismay and amusement. A few burst into applause, but the director had already reached the limousine that was to take him home.

Every time he tells this story, Auster laughs heartily, and it has never been entirely clear to me whether he is primarily amused or moved. "I don't know myself," he tells me, in his handsome brownstone near Prospect Park, in Brooklyn, "but I know that that's the only way Wilder could have ended his career."

You don't think it reveals a cynical attitude?
Perhaps. But I admire people who are able to make fun of themselves. Only a confident person is capable of doing that. And Wilder was certainly confident.

I wanted to mention the Wilder story in order to talk about religion.
Why do you keep wanting to talk about that?

Because it's the most important subject there is. If there is a God, how does he speak to us? And how do we speak to him?
I understand, but I'm sure that you can talk about God and religion even if you're not talking about them directly.

I'm sure of that, too, provided it's not a way of avoiding the problem or of making oneself a god in one's own image and likeness. So let me start our conversation by referring to what you've created in your books and films. Don't tell me there is no spiritual yearning in Smoke.

I would speak of a possibility of redemption, but not nec-
essarily of religion.

*I was very struck also by the elegiac tone of your most recent
book,* The Brooklyn Follies, *a novel in which there is a lot of
suffering, and yet what prevails is a humanity marked equally by
grace and by piety. The protagonist, the sixty-year-old Nathan
Glass, decides to return to the neighborhood of his childhood with
the intention of "finding a quiet place to die," after a terrible illness
and the failure of his marriage, but he rediscovers the mysterious joy
of existence.*

I have no problem calling *The Brooklyn Follies* a story of
regeneration and redemption, even though I'm well aware
of the recent abuse of these terms. I felt the need to tell a
bittersweet story, a comedy with dark aspects that, I hope,
offers a picture of contemporary existence that even those
who don't know Brooklyn can identify with.

Can we call it a human comedy?
Yes, of course.

What is your definition of comedy?
A story in which the characters are in a better place at the
end than they were at the beginning. Think of Shakespeare:
The conflicts in the tragedies and the comedies are nearly

identical, but their resolutions are entirely different. In the tragedies, everyone winds up dead on the stage. In the comedies, everyone gets married.

That's also the path of the Commedia *of Dante, which starts in the Inferno and ends in Paradise.*

Yes, but I still don't see a mystical or spiritual end point. At least in my own case.

Let's get to the basic question: do you think God exists?

No. I don't believe in him. But that doesn't mean that I don't consider religion a fundamental element of existence.

Were you brought up in a religious environment?

My parents were not particularly observant Jews, but until the age of fourteen I went to synagogue, and I remember my bar mitzvah with a kind of tenderness.

Then what happened?

I went through a crisis typical for people of that age.

How did you react?

I decided to confront the situation head on, and I went to talk to the rabbi. We met every week for several months. I found him very sympathetic, a man of integrity. He understood my state of mind and didn't condemn me for my rejection. Even now, I feel enormous respect for him.

How did your parents react?

With similar respect for my choices. But, I repeat, they were never real believers. My family belonged to that generation of Jews who came to religion after the war with an attitude that displayed above all a paradoxical sense of guilt. After the terrible sufferings of the Holocaust, many felt the need to draw closer to their roots.

Do you miss something of that reality?

There are things we miss in every choice we make. But I can't say I have regrets, and I'm sure I did the right thing.

Why did you call religion a fundamental element of existence?

Because only an ignorant person would say the opposite. Look at history, and what other conclusion can you come to?

In The Brooklyn Follies *there is a moment when the protagonist declares, "Give me a wily rascal over a pious sap any day of the week," using as an example the victory of Jacob over Esau.*

It's one of the passages of the Bible that most distressed me. It's not a principle I share, but it makes a certain sense. I think God wants to reward Jacob's courage.

What is it that, starting when you were fourteen, no longer seemed convincing to you?

The fact that there existed an omnipotent being responsible for all of creation. Obviously men didn't create the universe. But whatever force did, it's quite a leap to assume it was the work of a conscious being. But I also had—and continue to have—many problems with organized religion.

Do you think there is something negative about it?

Not in itself. Yet I believe that religions are stained, all religions. Think of how many times the name of God has been invoked to conquer or kill. Think of the Inquisition, of the expulsion of the Jews from Spain, or of the conflicts between Hindus and Muslims. The fundamentalist tendency of religion today frightens me, and I see around me a world filled with more and more fanatics. The problem of absolutism is that it leads you to believe that you own the truth. If you start from this assumption, you open the door to every sort of distortion, and you dehumanize whoever doesn't share your beliefs.

This may be true for fanatics; but Christianity, for example, asks us to love our neighbor and even turn the other cheek.

Of course, but abominations have been committed by Christians, too, or at least by people who think they are Christians. I'm not doubting the many positive effects that religion can have, but I can't help being aware of the evil effects as well.

What are the positive effects that you appreciate most?

The comfort it can bring to those who are frightened in the face of suffering or mystery. But this aspect also carries the risk of delusion.

In both Smoke *and* The Brooklyn Follies *the families of the protagonists are, to put it mildly, wrecks: there are drug addicts, a girl who becomes an actress in pornographic films, someone who out of spite cuts himself off from his relatives. And yet the family still has value.*

Many families are disasters, but that doesn't mean there aren't genuine lifelong bonds between the members of those families. I would be the last to deny the value of the family.

Do any of your characters follow a path similar to that of the protagonist of a book or film that is explicitly inspired by a religious belief?

Frankly, I had never thought about that. Give me an example.

At the beginning of The Brooklyn Follies, *Nathan is searching for "a silent end to my sad and ridiculous life," while at the end he proclaims himself "the happiest man who ever lived." From the point of view of an inner journey, is that any different from what happens to George Bailey in* It's a Wonderful Life?

Yes. Because Nathan's declaration of happiness comes on the morning of September eleventh, a few minutes before the terrorist attacks.

Capra's film doesn't at all rule out pain or new tragedies.

I know, but he was a Catholic, and he believed in grace and providence. I, on the other hand, see in the coupling of Nathan's declaration of happiness and the imminence of tragedy a mocking and unfathomable mystery.

New York,
August 2005

SAUL BELLOW

I Believe in God but I Don't Bug Him

Saul Bellow is curious about the idea of talking about such a private matter as religion, but he agreed to do so on condition of reserving the right not to respond to certain questions. "There are subjects it is impossible to talk about," he explains with a deeply ironic severity, "but that doesn't mean discussion is pointless. Some themes require modesty, respect, I would say even fear, and the value of a conversation in which we can't undertake extended reflection or impose absolute sincerity is in danger of being undermined."

Why do you consider sincerity impossible?
Because we are able to be absolutely sincere only with

ourselves and, in fact, with God. In an interview, even when there is complete good faith, narcissism, the wish to say something intelligent, and anxiety about how one will appear prevail in the end.

And why do you not consider even extended reflection possible?
Frankly it seems to me a little antithetical to journalism.

So you might as well not speak . . .
I didn't say that. I think that awareness of these dangers and these limits can provide a possible interpretation with respect to a theme as important as the one we are trying to address.

In other words you're saying: "We offer the reader damaged goods, but if he is attentive he will perceive the hidden value."
Isn't it always like that with the press?

I hope not. Why did you agree to discuss your relationship with religion?
Because it's obviously a subject that I feel strongly about and think about. And because I am fascinated by the fact that recently there has been a lot of talk about God, about religion, about spirituality, about the soul. In the last century these ideas seemed destined to disappear. Do you recall

everyone saying "God is dead"? Well, the only thing that is dead is those ideas.

Do you believe in God?
Yes.

And how do you imagine him?
I don't want to talk about that. I'm afraid of banality, and I think it's a subject whose importance is diminished by conversation.

Did you have a religious upbringing?
As you know, I'm Jewish. My mother was extremely religious while my father avoided the subject. I've often wondered if in reality this concealed an unresolved problem, and I'll confess to you that I've never reached a definite conclusion. I would say that he was an extremely skeptical person who fluctuated continually between distress regarding the possible existence of God and the choice of agnosticism. I can tell you in all sincerity that in the end it was my mother who had the greater influence on me.

There are Bible scholars who maintain that atheists don't exist: there are only believers and idolaters.

That's an interesting point, which has enormous potential to be provocative. I wonder how a person who declares himself an atheist might react to a statement of that sort: if the obligatory inference is that his conviction is false, then he has the right to be offended, leaving aside the fact that the principle may be true. The atheist has to be free to be what he wants. I think that's an important religious principle.

The Christian idea of grace is based on just this type of freedom.
I know the principle you mean: No one is beyond the reach of God. And I feel that I share it.

T. S. Eliot described himself as "classicist in literature, royalist in politics, and Anglo-Catholic in religion."
I don't much love classifications, especially those having to do with myself. You've reminded me of a journalist who asked me if I thought that I had been awarded the Nobel Prize as an American writer or as a Jewish writer.

What did you say?
That it had been awarded to me as a writer.

A few years ago, Frederick Glaysher wrote that you are the only American writer, along with Isaac Bashevis Singer, who addresses the problem of the modern soul.

That's another subject I prefer not to talk about: what I have to say is written in my books.

In Mr. Sammler's Planet *the protagonist declares, "Very often, and almost daily, I have strong impressions of eternity."*

There are moments when God shadows existence. And he persists in this manifestation. If you're looking for revelatory bits in what I've written I can help you: In another passage of the book I write that "the purest human beings, from the beginning of time, have understood that life is sacred," and if I remember correctly I refer more than once to the will of God.

But in Herzog *you write, "History is the history of cruelty, not love, as soft men think. . . . If the old God exists he must be a murderer."*

I could answer that Herzog is a literary character. But I want to tell you I believe that a man's life is also made of moments of desperation and rage. And it has to include a continuous reflection on this mystery: Herzog reflects on mankind's constant abominations, but that never interrupts his own relations with God.

The continuous probing of these subjects is a characteristic of many of your books. Do you think that the presence of spiritual themes represents an enrichment or a limitation in art?

It depends on the artist. If the approach is propagandistic, it immediately becomes a problem, whether the intent is to propagandize the existence or the absence of a spiritual reality.

You have always declared your great love for Conrad and Stendhal. Is there a writer you particularly like in whom religious themes are dominant?

Dostoyevsky, which brings us back to your previous question. His relationship with faith was genuine and unshakable, but it was useful to his art, and the torments of his characters never have the weight or futility of propaganda.

In an interview with The Boston Globe *you said, "I pray, but I don't believe in petition prayers: My requirements are trivial. I don't bug God."*

That's still true, but I would like to explain that I consider prayer above all an act of gratitude for existence.

But you don't believe that if God exists he is also a father whom we can bug?

Personally I see prayer as an intimate checkup with the headquarters of the universe.

What do you think happens at death?

This I don't know, but I don't think everything is resolved with the destruction of the body. What science has to say seems to me insufficient and unsatisfying.

BROOKLINE, MASSACHUSETTS,
JANUARY 2002

MICHAEL CUNNINGHAM

———

We Are All God's Children

Among the many people I encountered on this journey, Michael Cunningham is the one who most promptly agreed, and with the greatest enthusiasm, to talk about his relationship with religion and spirituality, but he also asked most explicitly for a guarantee that he would be able to check his own answers. I must admit that I got to know his writing through the film *The Hours,* which was based on his celebrated novel. And I had to overcome many prejudices. The film didn't work for me (perhaps because of Nicole Kidman's false nose) and only when I read the book afterward was I able to perceive the genuine power of the writer; in particular I was struck by the profound and painful humanity of his characters. The idea of openly discussing this intimate subject originated precisely in his apparent comprehension of suffering, which perhaps revealed a yearning for something transcendent on the part of characters who are conscious of being all too human.

This interview took place in two phases, during the renovation of Cunningham's apartment in New York.

Do you believe in God?

Well, we're starting off with the big one, aren't we? The sterner part of me, the part that's determined to be nobody's fool, says, "Just admit it. God is a fiction we've invented to help us live with our awareness of our own mortality." Dogs and cats think they will live forever, and have no god. I can't help but notice that the only species that knows from the get-go that it will one day no longer be alive is the one that erects cathedrals and marches around with statues dressed in robes.

But at the same time a universe with no ordering intelligence of any kind is so barren. I wonder if some of us aren't too smart for our own good on the subject. It's easy, especially in this late age, to congratulate yourself on your ability to see through everything, but when you see through everything you end up with nothing at all. Do I, does anyone, really and truly want to be so undeluded as to live in a world wholly devoid of mystery and magic?

When I was a kid I had a Magic 8-Ball. It was a plastic ball, like a billiard ball but the size of a grapefruit, and when you asked it a question and then shook it, one of, like, eight answers loomed up through a little violet-colored window at the bottom. One of them was "Reply hazy, try again later." I'm going to quote my childhood oracle, the Magic 8-Ball, on this one. Reply hazy, try again later.

Or, okay, to approach the question from a slightly more adult standpoint—I suspect there are profound and as yet undiscovered relationships between God and the principles of physics. And I do believe in physics.

Do you think that science can explain everything?

I don't think science, religion, art, or any other human pursuit can explain everything. But I do think they're all working toward the same end. One of the long-held goals of physics is the search for a unified field theory—an explanation of how the universe works that takes into account both astrophysics and the physics of subatomic particles, which at this point seem to be at odds with each other. What's true about the motion of stars does not turn out to be true of the motion of electrons and such, though that seems, and probably is, impossible. Scientists are working through mysteries as obscure and frustrating as those of theologians and artists, and a lot of what physicists are discovering right now doesn't really add up, doesn't make sense. So if you believe in physics, it's really not a big jump to say you believe in God. Some sort of god.

Tertullian said: "Credo quia absurdum" ("I believe because it is absurd").

That's a good paradox. Someone else, I can't remember who, said something like: "You might as well believe, because if you do and it turns out that you were right, you've had a life of faith and, depending on your convictions, maybe even the prospect of heavenly reward. And if it turns out you were wrong, that there's no god and no life after death, what have you really lost?" I like seeing it put so pragmatically. You could call it the smart shopper's approach to religion.

Tell me about your religious education.

I was brought up, nominally, in the Episcopal Church.

Why do you say nominally?

Because for us religion was all about going to church on Sundays and saying grace before dinner. I went to Sunday school as a kid, I can recite the Nicene Creed and all, but our house as I was growing up was uninvaded by any active sense of Christian spirituality. We didn't have crucifixes or statues of the Blessed Virgin or anything like that. You could probably say we went to church because it would have seemed too strange not to.

But, you know, oddly, as a kid I was obsessed with Christian iconography. My relatives on my mother's side were all Catholic—maybe that's where it came from. I made communion wafers out of Wonder Bread. And I did these religious paintings when I was, like, seven or eight or so. The one I considered my masterpiece involved souls rising up out of a cemetery and ascending to Heaven. They were all in white gowns, and all their faces were in profile, because profiles were all I could draw. They were smiling ecstatically and floating up toward Heaven, which I'd painted in the upper-right-hand corner of the canvas and covered with gold glitter. As I recall, my depiction of Heaven looked very much like the Griffith Observatory. That's in the hills in Los Angeles, where I grew up. It's where Sal Mineo gets shot in *Rebel Without a Cause.*

Then, when I got a little older, I had a friend who went to Catholic school. The hallways of her school were all hung with musty old tapestries, and near the entrance to the cafeteria stood a life-size white sculpture of Christ, holding his robe open to reveal his bright red, bleeding heart. Right, every day on their way to the fish sticks and Tater Tots, the girls were marched past Jesus, quietly bleeding for them. Behind the playground there was a field of black iron crosses, where the nuns were buried. Now, my public high school looked more or less like a strip mall in decline. I so envied the spookiness of my friend's school. It seemed like part of a more mysterious, creepy, but promising world.

Are you saying that Catholicism gave you a stronger sense of the presence of God than Episcopalianism?
Let's say the implied presence of that particular scary God was more compelling to me than the general aura of dusty secular defeat that drifted around my own school.

What is the image you have of God?
She's black.

You know that Derek Walcott told me he still imagines him as an old, bearded white man?
I suppose these images arrive pretty early. When I was very young I had a babysitter, a big black woman I loved extravagantly. When I think of God, I think of her.

Do you think that organized religion can approach God?
Let's say I don't think organized religion is doing a very good job of it right now. So much of what's seriously fucked up in the world extends directly from organized religion, whether it's murderous fundamentalists or the Pope declaring that gay men can no longer be priests, whether they're celibate or not.

There's a big difference between organized religion and fundamentalism. There are so many forms of organized religion and fundamentalism. It'd be silly to try and generalize about something so vast and complicated. I do think the very idea of dogma—the notion that I'm right and by definition other people are wrong—opens the door to the kind of extremism that clearly seems to be the most dangerous force in the world today.

Do you think that religion in politics represents an opportunity or a danger?

I don't think religions should govern countries. Religions are singular, populations are diverse. I am so totally down with the separation of church and state.

What do you like about religions and what can't you accept?

As far as I know, most religions teach fundamental principles of behavior with which I agree entirely. The sanctity of life, compassion for others, charity to the less fortunate. On the other hand, one can't help noticing how much of the savagery out there is being committed in the name of religion. We're talking here about people who are willing to commit murder to save the life of a fetus and at the same time support the death penalty. Apparently it's a sin to kill them when they're in utero, but okay to do it later on.

The definition of the sanctity of every phase of life seems to me a clear reference to abortion. What's your position on that?

I'm in favor of the principle that every woman has the right to choose.

I'm sorry, but how do you reconcile that with the idea of the sanctity of every moment of life?

I don't believe the fetus has consciousness in the initial stages of its evolution.

In those phases, is the fetus a something or a someone?

If it has no consciousness it isn't really someone.

Even when the freedom you speak of is placed before the defense of the principle of life?

Then we get to the question of when life begins, which has been thoroughly discussed. Not that we seem even close to agreeing about it. If nascent life is life, period, then doesn't birth control destroy life? It's a slippery slope that leads all the way back to the injunction against sex for any purpose other than procreation. I have no interest in returning to that era, thanks.

What do you think there is after life?

Every time I undergo a change, if I move, or leave someone, I think of it as practice for death. It's a mini-death, immediately followed by a mini-resurrection. You live on, but as someone in a new apartment, with a different lover. Your old self has in a sense died and been replaced by this new self.

I suspect we go on, but without our consciousnesses. And that feels to us like extinction, just as surely as, say, leaving someone with whom we've lived for a decade can feel like extinction. It's not—it's just the end of one thing and the beginning of something else. Like most people, I'm extremely attached to my consciousness, my persona, my body of habits and all. But at the same time I ask myself: Do I really want to be attached to all that forever? If I did continue as an individual, would I be eternally ten years old? Twenty-eight? Seventy-five? I like to think that something of myself will remain and will unite with other elements in the universe. Maybe that's what believers refer to as the soul.

Some theologians maintain that there are no atheists but only believers and idolaters.

Where would that leave, say, social revolutionaries? You can believe passionately in something larger than yourself, like the good of your people, without having any faith in any kind of god. Che Guevara was not an idolater, nor was Emma Goldman.

You don't think that, for example, in the case of Che Guevara, the idol is represented by the revolution?

If dedicating your life to bettering the world is idolatry, then I say, fuck everything.

Can art help one reach God?

The greatest art can reflect some element of the divine. Think of Rilke or Rothko. On this one, the Magic 8-Ball would say "Signs point to yes."

What artists do you admire in whom you feel a strong religious presence?

Most prominently, Flannery O'Connor. She was an utterly orthodox Catholic, and one of the greatest writers of the twentieth century. What's more, you can't separate her faith from her art, though some critics have tried. If you insist on reading her and treating her Catholicism as some sort of obstacle she managed to overcome, you not only miss the point of what she was doing but insult her memory. O'Connor, in her fiction and in her letters and essays, is the best argument I know against dismissing Catholicism outright. As she said more than once, her belief informed and clarified her vision. I have no doubt that that was true.

In the figure of Christ do you see a great thinker or the son of God?

I see a great thinker and philosopher. We are all children of God.

How do you see a believer? Someone deluded? Ingenuous? A person blessed by grace? Or someone who lives a mysterious experience and deserves respect?

I think that anyone who believes in anything other than shopping is a hero. I admire every form of nonviolent reverence.

NEW YORK,
NOVEMBER 2005

NATHAN ENGLANDER

Whoever Wrote the Bible Is God

When Nathan Englander agrees to speak about his personal relationship with religion, he has been working on the translation into Hebrew of his short-story collection *For the Relief of Unbearable Urges.* The mixture of love and rebelliousness that characterizes his relationship with Jerusalem and Jewish culture, and the controversies raised by the book within the Orthodox community, kept him from translating it into the language of his ancestors. Four years after its publication, having returned to live in America, he has finally decided to do the translation, and he has begun the work with the patient precision of someone who attributes to words an absolute, religious value. We meet on the day of his thirty-third birthday. He has decided to cut his hair, which falls below his shoulders. "At thirty-three," he says, "only Jesus can be forgiven for having hair this long." The tone in which he utters the sentence is less joking than ironic, and, as in his stories, the irony reveals an intimate and difficult relationship with religion, which seems far from being resolved.

I didn't expect to begin this conversation with Christ.

Why, do you think he's the exclusive property of Christians?

No, not at all. But it's not exactly the first reference that one expects from someone who's written a book like yours and was brought up according to the rigid dictates of Orthodox Judaism.

I can answer you that both in the book and in life I've tried to reject every religious absolutism. And I've discovered that life is more confusing than I could have imagined when living within a traditional black-and-white world. In that gray space, while educating myself, I did my best to read broadly. And for a Jewish kid from suburbia, Christianity would fall into that category.

Are you telling me that you're converting to Christianity?

Not at all. Only that I try to look at everything that surrounds me with a level gaze, including other religions. As far as Catholicism is concerned, I wanted to learn about

Vatican II. I've always been interested in the link between Jews and Christians. When Pope John Paul II visited the synagogue in Rome, he called the Jews "our older brothers." It's a definition that in some ways sounds nice, but it also indicates a division. And I don't know if it can be otherwise. For me, it brings to mind the notion of the conflict between an Israel of the Spirit and an Israel of the Flesh.

How did your parents react to your decision to abandon Orthodox Judaism?

I felt that they were supportive, even though I understood that it must have been a real trauma for them. And for my sister as well, who is still very observant.

Your collection of stories was extraordinarily successful everywhere but was also greeted by many polemics on the part of the Orthodox community.

The first was a happy surprise, but not the second. My stories try to represent the confusion I feel with respect to teachings that revolve around a religious, and in many cases also a political, assumption.

How would you define your current relationship with religion?

That of a person who's stripped off everything, who feels freed up by it but perhaps doesn't always know what to do about the naked part.

But do you believe in God?

I'd be inclined to say no if I didn't fear God's wrath.

You went to live in Jerusalem, but then you chose America again.

The motivation was mainly political. In Israel I found myself observing daily that my opinions were automatically on the extreme left. To many it will seem paradoxical, but here in America I feel less critical toward Israel, and at the same time I have a greater sense of freedom. I returned a little before September eleventh and I learned to love New York in a new way then: I'm very proud of my city.

The tragic conflicts going on now have their roots in religion.

In fundamentalism, which is precisely what I reject. I think that fundamentalism is like alcoholism: an extremely dangerous excess. I left Israel when I saw in Sharon and Arafat the same type of self-destructive attitude. I know perfectly well that we could talk for a long time about the extremism that is also present in this country, about the fact that it's absurd even linguistically to speak of a war on terror and on extremists, but here in America there is, first of all, the religion of freedom. And this is the reason that I have trouble accepting certain references to God made by those who govern this country.

Your childhood was marked by strict spiritual teachings.

I can tell you that at the time I believed that this was faith. For hours I would mechanically repeat the prayers that I still know by heart today, but I didn't understand their meaning. The moment came when I realized that for me it was only a ritual.

Do you still read the Holy Scriptures?

Of course I read them. The Bible is easily the most beautiful work ever written; whoever wrote it is God to me.

Do you know the New Testament as well?

Not like the Old, but I much like the beginning of the Gospel according to John: "In the beginning was the Word, and the Word was with God, and the Word was God."

Do you say that as a writer or as a man of faith?

Sometimes I wonder if there is a difference. But if you mean to ask what remains in me of the boy brought up on the Scriptures, I can tell you that when I close the Bible I kiss it and I'm careful about where I place it in my library.

What fascinates you particularly about the Bible?

Its complexity, and its capacity to speak in the language of eternity.

You've been working on a novel for five years, and for you the written word has fundamental importance.

I have the greatest respect for it. When it comes to writing I have an intransigent, inflexible, absolutist approach.

In other words, you've ended up in another type of fundamentalism.

I accept the provocation, but I know that despite that attitude I have just enough control to keep myself from slipping into fanaticism. I would say that I behave like a monk who is trying to resist intolerance within himself. And I hope never to be like those people you see who—in the space of a short time—go from being sex addicts to being drug addicts, and then suddenly you see them in the synagogue wearing a yarmulke and calling on God.

Can you tell me a religious writer you particularly like?

There are many: the first who comes to mind is Isaac Bashevis Singer, for his mixture of carnality and spirituality. But I find a profound spirituality in Kafka, and even in Gogol. Yesterday evening I spent an hour on the phone with Donald Antrim talking about how some writers conceal a yearning for spirituality and maybe divinity in themes that seem to speak only of human frailty or of the corruption of the soul.

Luis Buñuel said that he was "an atheist by the grace of God."

I share that feeling, and I'm ready to steal the remark.

Do you believe in life after death?

It's a question that brings me to a point of crisis. Yet again I would be tempted to say no, that it's an illusion and also perhaps a joke, but if you ask me where I think my grandfather is at this moment I would answer: in Paradise.

NEW YORK,
FEBRUARY 2003

JANE FONDA

Christ Was the First Feminist

There are few things that Jane Fonda repents of having done in sixty-nine years of life, but she has many regrets about how she carried out some of her more controversial actions and choices and, especially, about how those choices have been interpreted. She assumes all the responsibility herself, and at the same time looks back with pride at the strength she has demonstrated in difficult moments, of which there have been many, going back to her early childhood. She is still very beautiful and has the tough bearing of one who has seen a lot, but behind the assurance with which she answers the most personal questions she reveals a disarming will to follow her own interior journey, in the painful knowledge that every day she falls down and picks herself up again. I met her through a mutual friend, the producer Paula Weinstein, and probably I owe to this introduction Fonda's generosity toward me and her willingness to talk even about very intimate subjects. "I'm used to everything—ask me whatever is helpful to you," she says. "And I'll be happy to talk about God."

In her autobiography, entitled *My Life So Far,* she recounts her mistakes and insights, her traumas and successes, and certainly it's not just coincidence that many of the chapters are preceded by religious quotations. Having reached what she calls her "third act," she decided to talk about her troubled relationship with her father, Henry, an American icon; the trauma of the death of her mother; her serious problems with anorexia and bulimia; the failure of her three marriages; her passionate political activism and the controversial trip to Vietnam; her period as an exercise guru; and her conversion to Christianity. "I discovered the grandeur of the Christian universe quite recently," she tells me, looking me in the eye, "and I'm still amazed by how much ignorance there is about it—an ignorance that until a few years ago I also shared."

What is it that appealed to you in the Christian message to the point that you converted?

The sublime teachings, but also something I realized I had been looking for since childhood. I think that Christ was the first feminist, and because of that I've learned from his teachings to call myself a Christian feminist.

What do you mean?

That the feminist consciousness is utterly compatible with Christian teaching, and no one has been able to celebrate the greatness of women as Christ did. In recent years I've been an eager student of the Scriptures, and I wanted to deepen my knowledge of the Apocryphal Gospels as well, in particular the Coptic gospel attributed to St. Thomas, where, in chapter 22, it says that to enter the Kingdom of Heaven one must be "male and female . . . a single one, so that the male will not be male nor the female be female." I think that the lack of this equilibrium represents one of the great problems of modernity.

Your adherence to the Christian faith isn't orthodox—you've just quoted the Apocryphal Gospels.

I think they contain marvelous and enlightening passages. The first Christians considered themselves seekers rather than believers, a condition I feel a strong affinity with.

Did your parents give you a religious upbringing?

My mother died when I was a child, and my father was an atheist. He called religion a crutch, something useful to support people with weak convictions.

What, then, is religion for you?

I consider it not a matter of traditions and dogmas but, rather, a spiritual experience. I'd like to return to the discussion of the feminism of Christ: I think that his teaching revolutionized the idea of Eve being born from Adam's rib, as if God had rethought it. In my opinion, that idea was used to justify centuries of misogyny. Christ's position is absolutely new: the friendship he showed for women is truly revolutionary, and it's certainly not coincidental that it was women who responded most passionately to his message of compassion, love, and total equality.

You haven't mentioned redemption.

But of course I think about it. And I also want to add that since I began studying the Scriptures and the history of Christianity I've been constantly making extraordinary discoveries. For example, in the early Christian communities there were more women than men.

In the first pages of your autobiography you assert that discipline represents freedom. It's surprising to hear a statement like that from someone like you, someone who has fiercely resisted institutions.

It's a principle I learned from Martha Graham, and for many years it seemed to me absurd and contradictory. Today I see its profound wisdom. To stick with the example of dance, I think it was discipline that made it possible for

Nureyev to seem to hover in the air. And I think that the concepts of freedom and discipline have to start with the necessity of knowing yourself and your own demons.

Would you talk about your mother in relation to your life choices?

My mother, Frances Ford Seymour, killed herself when I was twelve. She suffered from what's now called bipolar disorder, and she tried to get better by deciding to recover on her own. She didn't make it. It's she who gave me life, and she gave me strength to bear the pain of the wounds it inflicted on me.

The book in which you tell about your commitment to Christianity is full of religious references, ranging from the Gospel of St. Matthew to Ecclesiastes, but there are also quotations of another type—for example, from Hannah Arendt.

I've always been fascinated by what she says about the past, that if you don't know history, you are condemned to live it as if it were a personal destiny. We are the product of our parents and their forebears. Only by knowing their history will we be able to understand who we are. For example, I know that each of my failures and successes has an indissoluble link with my family. And I'm referring also to the past, including my family's long-ago origins, in Genoa.

You acknowledge that you have made many mistakes. But what do you regret?

I should have been a better mother to my daughter. Perhaps at the root of this failing is the fact that I never loved myself enough, and didn't feel equal to it. I would like to say that I've been working hard to reestablish a relationship that for me is fundamental.

In the story of your marriage to Roger Vadim, you speak explicitly of the sexual relations à trois *that your husband forced you into.*

I can tell you that I'm sorry not for what I did but for how I did it: I accepted his will without letting my own voice be heard. To feel loved and to show that I loved him, I betrayed myself and my body.

Do you consider it a sin?

To the degree that I've just said.

What are the achievements that you are most proud of in your sixty-nine years of life?

I think I have children I can call successful human beings. As far as I'm concerned, having developed a social conscience, having been at times courageous and always curious. I've learned that it's much more important to be interested than interesting.

Do you think you've been courageous in your religious choice?

I don't know if one can consider faith an act of courage, but certainly it's an experience that changes every element of existence.

Plato said, "Kalos gar o kindynos," "Risk is beautiful," to explain the irrational choice of faith.

That's a definition in which I see myself, and I find it particularly appealing. I think it's something totally personal. As for myself, I've been diligent about my relationship with religion, and I do serious Bible study.

It's clear from what you've been telling me that you admire and venerate the figure of Christ, but perhaps it would be useful to go more deeply into your position regarding the Church.

I have problems with religious institutions, and I continue to believe that churches have enforced or censored certain teachings for political rather than religious motives. It's one of the reasons that I believe in the so-called Apocryphal Gospels.

The Church has never condemned those texts.

Nor has it encouraged them, and, in the case of a text like the secret book of Mark, it was in fact suppressed in the fourth century, because of the concept that having experience of the divine is more important than simple faith in the divine.

Much of the debate about the Apocryphal Gospels that you've cited, and the consequent establishment of the canon, has to do with the fact that, while some of these texts are certainly pious, they are rife with elements that originate simply in tradition. Just think of the famous story of the palms that bow down before Jesus. These are devotional elements, while for those who believe in the Gospel the good news is what leads to salvation.

I think that each of us has to experience this element within ourself, in independence and freedom. And I think that passages like the ones I quoted about equilibrium between the two sexualities are illuminating.

Probably the greatest theological conflict within Christianity has been the relationship between faith and works. For example, there's the letter of St. James, in which he claims that faith without works has no value. Whereas Luther and, after him, the Protestants do not consider it Holy Scripture.

As far as I'm concerned works are fundamental, and personally I try to do something every day that improves the existence of people who suffer. But I think that the relation between faith and the experience of the divine is no less important.

Isn't there the danger of an attitude that is too vague and New Age?

I'm aware of the danger, but to say that Jesus is the only way to salvation has an odor of Christian imperialism.

And if I say to you, "Extra ecclesiam nulla salus" ("There is no salvation outside the Church")?

I would answer that maybe it isn't the spiritual house I'm looking for.

ROME,
OCTOBER 2005

RICHARD FORD

I Believe in the Redemptiveness of Art

When I ask Richard Ford if he would be willing to discuss his personal relationship with God and religion, he immediately says, "But don't you know I'm an agnostic?" I explain to him that this changes nothing, and is in fact an element of, a way of enriching, the discussion, and he says that he wants a couple of days before giving me a definite answer. He calls me back from his car, saying that he's spending a few days in Riverdale, in the Bronx, where he and his wife, Kristina, recently bought a house. He was sorry he had accepted a teaching job ("The classes can be stimulating, but the rest of academic life is a nightmare"), and wanted to spend the spring break as far away as possible from the campus. "Yes, I decided it might be interesting to chat about the Eternal Father," he says to me in an ironic tone, "but I want to come to your house. I don't know why, but I think it would be more interesting to tackle a subject like that in a place I don't know well." He comes to see me on a bright day of winter sunshine, and looks out at the clear blue sky for a long time, commenting simply, "It's a glorious day." Standing at the window, with his solemn gaze turned to the crystalline beauty of America, he seems the very personification of his country, and the energy of his smile and the wish to confront immediately a subject as unexpected as it is fundamental demonstrate that he is the first to be aware of it. "So shall we begin?" He sits down in an armchair from which he can go on looking out the window. "I'm ready."

Then let's get right to the point: do you believe in God, Richard?
No.

Have you ever believed?
On the contrary: I was brought up in a religious manner, and until I was twenty-one went to church regularly.

Tell me about your family background.
In terms of religion, my upbringing was Protestant. The Fords come from the southern part of Ulster, an area of harsh, violent conflicts. One of my great-grandfathers was a

minister, and my parents were both very religious. My mother was partly educated in a school run by Catholic nuns. In spite of that, I was brought up according to the dictates of Presbyterianism, and when I was a child, in Mississippi, besides the Sunday service I went to a service Wednesday evening and also to choir practice.

Then what happened?

I began to feel increasingly uneasy: I seemed to be performing mechanical rituals. Religion was giving me nothing.

You don't think that religion means to give as well as to receive?

Of course, but I think that receiving or feeling something that changes one's existence still represents a crucial aspect of it. As for myself, I didn't feel the leap that faith should offer, only an empty and meaningless ritual.

When did the turning point come?

I have a precise memory: I was twenty-one and was in college in Michigan. I was going to church, as I did every Sunday, and suddenly I asked myself what was the meaning of it. I felt an impulse of disillusion and rebellion.

Could we say that your religion is writing?

Absolutely yes, and I want to emphasize that the two choices are closely linked. I recall clearly the sensation that ever since I was a child I had been trying every means, had sought every opportunity to believe.

What you describe testifies to a yearning.
It is, and it has been satisfied by reading and writing.

What does death represent to you?
The end. I hope not to realize at that moment that I've been totally wrong. But it would be too late anyway.

Religion teaches that it's never too late.
I don't deny that a part of me might say that to myself. But it's not a subject that I worry about: my religion, and my reason for living, is in art. I want to quote a phrase of Wallace Stevens that I always keep in mind: "In an age of disbelief it is for the poet to supply the satisfaction of belief in his measure and in his style."

But is it an illusion or is it something real or salvific?
I believe in the redemptiveness of art, and I also want to quote a marvelous passage from the second letter of St. Paul to the Hebrews: "Faith is the substance of things hoped for, the evidence of things unseen."

How do you now look at the years of adolescence when you were a believer?

I can't even say with certainty that I was a believer.

What is your opinion of Dostoyevsky's assertion "If God doesn't exist, then everything is permitted"?

It's a profound ethical formulation, but it can't be the only one. I continue to think that redemption can take other forms: Henry James maintained that "it is art that makes life, makes interest, makes importance."

Do you feel the need for a common, shared ethics?

Of course, but I don't feel the need for something that comes from the outside. I remember trying to pray and feeling with frustration that my body never felt lighter. I won't conceal the fact that I'm happy to have freed myself from religion.

What do you feel toward those who do believe? Do you consider them deluded, deceived?

I won't say that: I consider that people have to determine their own spiritual choices. But I don't have much respect for institutionalized religion. On too many occasions I've seen bigoted attitudes that tend toward exclusion. And I see the corruption of money.

Art has plenty of that, too, but it doesn't jeopardize its importance.

That is corruption, not the essence: art is free.

One could say the same of religion.

That's true, but its expectations and its claims imply a sacredness that is too often betrayed. To return to your question about believers, I see them solely as free human beings.

Among writers who have treated religious themes, do you like any in particular?

Chaucer, but also, or perhaps especially, for his satiric approach. And J. F. Powers and Graham Greene, although Greene is less interesting when he speaks too explicitly about religion and everything is resolved in the conflict between body and spirit.

Yet it's Christ himself who says, "The spirit is willing, but the flesh is weak."

I know, but it's probably the concept of God that's alien to me. While you continue to press me on these subjects I continue to think about art, and how I identify it with divinity. It's said that God is in the details. Or maybe it's the Devil who's in the details. I always get those confused. But I think the same can be said of art.

How would you explain the religious revival that seems to have invaded every part of the world?

I don't know if there is a single explanation. What immediately comes to mind is the charisma of certain religious leaders, obviously combined with the eternal need for answers. I wonder, though, if it's a real revival or a constant, which perhaps we notice more in secularized societies. There is also politics, and the cynical and dangerous use that it makes of religion.

Do you share Marx's definition of religion as the opiate of the people?

No comment.

What do you mean?

That it's fine with me if someone wants to say it, but I wouldn't, in turn, make a religion of it, and I think it would also be right to assert the opposite.

NEW YORK,
MARCH 2005

PAULA FOX

———————

God Is the Name of Something
I Don't Understand

On a beautiful fall morning, Paula Fox greets me in her brownstone on Clinton Street in Brooklyn. Before leading me to her study, she takes me out to see the garden behind the house, which is overgrown but beautiful; she shows me some reproductions of views of Italian cities, and what she calls her gallery—photographs of people she loves, along with drawings done by her grandchildren. She moves easily, as if to belie her eighty-two years, and her exquis-itely gentle manner contrasts with convictions stated with a humble but steely firmness. She immediately agreed to dis-cuss her personal relationship with religion, and appears impressed by the choice of subject. "It's a subject that's very topical," she says with the smile of one who wants to know if she can trust her questioner, "but I have never talked about it directly in an interview. In general, one discusses books, politics, or much more superficial things."

Doesn't that seem odd to you?
Of course. But you can't underrate the fact that it's a private matter.

And yet one can't deny it in public.
It's one thing to deny, another to live privately.

I think the moment has come to ask if you are a believer.
No, I'm not a believer. And above all I don't believe in the common image of God as a male.

Do you have a particular image?
Not being a believer, I can't have one, but I must add, still in answer to the preceding question, that I believe in mystery and beauty. And both things can find representation. I think that what is defined as God is the answer that each of us gives in obedience to an inner law.

Tell me about your religious upbringing.
My mother was a Cuban of Spanish origin who was directly descended from an agent of the Holy Inquisition named Felix del Camino. I think that this ancestor led

her to have an attitude of total detachment from faith and, in my case, made me hostile to every form of fundamentalism. My father was also an atheist, in spite of a Protestant upbringing, like my grandfather. But in both I recall qualities of solidarity and sharing that I would not hesitate to call spiritual.

What was your first encounter with religion?

I was reared until the age of five and a half by a Congregationalist minister. We lived in a big house on the Hudson, seventeen miles from the church, and I remember the drives to the place where he performed the religious services. He was a marvelous man and very entertaining, and I owe a lot to him. He let me play in his study while he was preparing his sermons, and I remember that once I managed to persuade him to speak in church about the power of waterfalls.

You didn't feel you believed even during that period when you went to church?

There was a point where I had a mystical infatuation, which lasted for several months. I was around ten, and had also begun to sing in the church choir, and then a stupid incident destroyed my enthusiasm: a boy stuck the pages of the scores together with chewing gum. I think that crisis was an obvious sign of the fact that my interest wasn't very serious. I recall that during that period I lived in a state of euphoria and happiness. But I can tell you that I've experienced that same state, whether or not I considered the presence of God.

What do you still like about religion?

I love the joy of forgiveness, of humility, and the understanding of human frailty. A few days ago I accidentally bumped into a man coming to make a delivery. When I apologized, he said to me, "Don't ever ask pardon. It's a sign of weakness." I don't know if he wanted to be nice and was trying not to make me feel embarrassed, but I think that such a concept reveals the lack of religious upbringing.

How did you react?

I tried to reply politely by saying to him, "On the contrary: asking pardon is a sign of strength." But I want to go on telling you what I love about religion: the churches and, in particular, cathedrals. And I love sacred art, especially of the sixteenth and seventeenth centuries. I can't listen to Bach without recalling that he was an organist and that most of his compositions are sacred. Listening to his music I feel a great joy. I was in Assisi recently, and I think it's impossible even for the most inveterate atheist not to feel something special and indefinable there. As for myself, when I visited the Porziuncola, with Mount Subasio opposite turning gold at sunset, I felt that I was in the presence of the mystery. Amid these sensations I say to myself that religion may represent the highest level of searching for an answer to the questions that existence places before us.

How do you see those who believe?

I have the greatest respect for them, as I have for all who seek. One of my best friends is a man who studied at a seminary, and although he decided not to become a priest, he never lost his faith. We have long conversations about the meaning of life, and I can't say that he is wrong. On the other hand, the reborn Christians and fundamentalists frighten me, attempting to impose their vision of the world and denying even the most obvious scientific truths. I think that their attitude is dangerous, and also far from religion.

For an atheist like you, what is a religious leader? An impostor?

No, absolutely not. For example, I have great esteem for the Dalai Lama. And I admired John Paul II enormously: in both I felt honesty and the force of their religious convictions. Of course, the history of every religion offers disastrous examples, and I don't even want to consider the sects that are proliferating in this country. But those have little to do with religion.

What do you think about artists in whom the religious element is essential?

I would say that among my favorite artists, in two completely different fields, are Flannery O'Connor and Doménikos Theotokópoulos—that is, El Greco. I find their total devotion to something that they thought of as superior to them moving.

You never had an image of God even in your brief "religious" period?

It was a completely vague image. Today I think that it's utterly disrespectful to personalize and make human something that we don't know and can't understand. In fact, I believe that everything is God: it's the name of something that I don't understand, that no one can understand. I believe that God, or what believers call God, is in every aspect of nature: in the giraffe, in my cat, Lucy, and even in cockroaches.

What will happen after death?

The future is made of ashes, worms, and bones. I think of the insight of Walt Whitman, in *Leaves of Grass,* about the generations that go before and those which follow. Personally I can't imagine a Paradise: although I feel sincere respect for those who believe, I think it's a childish idea.

Is there anything toward which you have an attitude of faith?

The truth. I think that seeking the truth is what makes life bearable. Some time ago, when I was correcting a manuscript, I had a flash of intuition, and from that moment I swore to myself that everything I produced would have to be sincere, including the articles and the conjunctions.

You live in a country where 90 percent of the population believes in God.

It's an extraordinary number, but I would submit to you another statistic, according to which 60 percent of Americans think that the sun goes around the earth.

Excuse me, but what does faith have to do with ignorance?

That's a legitimate question for a believer, but not for an atheist. To return to the question you asked, I consider myself at home in this neighborhood but a stranger in this country.

Do you think that the United States is experiencing a fundamentalist drift?

Drift may be an extreme term, but certainly militant faith has acquired a weight that it didn't have in the past, with obvious political and social consequences. And I would like to add that as an atheist I feel offended when I hear the name of God used too easily to justify and reinforce someone's convictions.

NEW YORK,
NOVEMBER 2005

JONATHAN FRANZEN

***

Reality Is an Illusion

Jonathan Franzen moved recently, but he didn't want to leave the Upper East Side. His new apartment has been constructed out of two apartments in an elegant apartment building just off Lexington Avenue, and is furnished in a minimalist style, with meticulous order. He greets me kindly and with embarrassment: "I'm afraid I don't have much to say about God." He looks as if he wished to correct the remark but drops the subject. He asks me about films I've seen recently, about some mutual friends, but then he decides that it's time to stop beating about the bush and confront the subject that I had mentioned to him in advance.

Let's begin with the key question: do you believe in God?

What do you mean by God? What's your definition?

An omnipotent being who created us.

[Franzen remains silent. He reflects, then shakes his head.]
The truth is, I don't have a precise answer.

What do you mean?

There's a part of me that believes in *something,* but there
are a lot of obvious problems with the idea of an omnipotent being. If we're talking about the classic image of God,
sitting up in Heaven pulling strings, the answer to your
question is clearly no.

Why don't we begin with your religious upbringing?

My father was a militant atheist, absolutely convinced of
the nonexistence of God, and yet he taught me to go to
church. He believed that the precepts of Christianity were a
good thing—that this was a doctrine that inspired good
actions. He also went to church and recognized its moral
authority. He believed that Jesus was a great man, even
though he saw him as a thinker and not the son of God.

*That brings to mind Benedetto Croce's maxim "We can't not
call ourselves Christians."*

Actually, my father's father was very good at not calling

himself a Christian. He was an atheist, like my father, but a lot more militant. He had no respect at all for religion. To him, it was basically just a fraud. He sent out Christmas letters every year in which he ridiculed people who believed in God. And then there was my mother, whose family was Catholic but who was very frank about not believing in anything supernatural.

What do you remember of your experience in church?

I went to a Congregational church in St. Louis for twelve years, and I was very involved in the youth fellowship for six years. But that was in the seventies, when you weren't required to see the Bible as anything but a collection of metaphors and great stories. What strikes me now, thirty years later, is how I never for a minute believed in God in the traditional sense. And yet at the same time I heard those great stories so early in my life that they're embedded in my brain, and even now I kind of half believe them. Part of me just *believes* that the Red Sea really did part, and that Jesus really did perform miracles, and that he rose from the dead. I wasn't there on the spot. I don't know everything. I can't honestly rule anything out.

But, Jonathan, this last assertion is rather startling. How can you think that resurrection is possible and not be a believer?

First of all, it occurs to me to say that these are very

beautiful stories, but I realize that that might just seem like a writer's response. Let's say that if God exists he works in a manner so mysterious that in the end it's almost irrelevant for me. But at the same time I would insist that part of me believes.

What image do you have of this God you believe in, even if only in part?

I don't have a definite idea. One thing I do know is that God's not like some chief executive sitting at a control panel, calling all the shots. I don't believe in a God that responds to prayers. At the same time, I think there's a reality beneath what we can see with our eyes and experience with our senses. There's ultimately something mysterious and unmaterialist about the world. Something large and awe-inspiring and eternal and unknowable. I'm not particularly mystical myself, but I have a lot of respect for the notion of a mystical experience. It's important to me to know that this is a possible dimension of the world.

Do you ever think about death?
Of course.

And do you see it as the end of everything or as a passage to something else?
I see it as a mystery. As *the* mystery. When I'm afraid, like

when I'm in an airplane in bad weather, I tell myself that if I die in a crash I'll be making the same crossing that my parents have already made. That I'll be going where they've already gone.

Let's go back in time. What was your idea of God at the time when you were going to church?

Even then it was somewhat indistinct, but it was something like Aslan, the lion in *The Chronicles of Narnia*. He's an incredibly strong animal, but he has this very sweet breath. He's terrifying, but if you trust him he can be comforting.

Aslan dies to save the world. Lewis makes him not only a divine figure but, more specifically, Christological.

Well, this goes to my idea that the Bible is full of great stories.

I've asked many of those I've interviewed to comment on Dostoyevsky's phrase "If God doesn't exist, everything is permitted."

What did others say?

I'd rather not tell you and let you answer without being influenced by them.

Dostoyevsky is obviously one of the giants of literature and he's one of my favorite writers. But I honestly think that he was wrong about this. Unless you make *God* so abstract that it's just a word for "an idea of goodness," I don't think our intrinsic moral sense depends on our avowing the existence of God.

Dostoyevsky suggests that this moral sense isn't sufficient, or at least that without the awareness of an omnipotent and paternal entity, man would be constantly committing atrocities.

People commit atrocities in the name of God as well.

Of course, but that seems to me the degeneration of a belief, or, if you like, the curse of belief itself. The other is, instead, an existence that does not contemplate entities and hence has no type of moral restraint except what is entrusted to the individual.

Dostoyevsky was a brilliant artist, and there's no question that he helped to expand our understanding of human beings as entities with all sorts of contradictory things happening inside all at once. But I think he was a better artist and psychologist than he was a philosopher or theologian.

What contemporary writers do you think most clearly display a religious spirit?

Don DeLillo comes immediately to mind, with his Jesuit education. In his last couple of novels he's a mystical writer. David Means and Denis Johnson also come to mind. On the opposite side, there's Alice Munro, who is totally in the Greek and pagan tradition.

One of the central themes of recent years has been the role of religion in politics.

I'm all for the separation of church and state, and there's a lot of ugly political stuff being done around the world in the name of various fundamentalisms. But it's important not to forget the positive role that religion has played in making the world a better place. Think, for example, of what happened in this country with abolitionism and then the battle for civil rights led by Martin Luther King, Jr., a great religious leader.

Let's stay with the subject of the separation of church and state. In your opinion, how should a person behave who wants to follow the dictates of his faith but is in a country that, for example, provides abortion or euthanasia by law?

Obviously, if you don't like the laws, you can work to try to change them. And for citizens who don't believe, it's probably a useful exercise to try to understand people who do believe.

What would you say to someone who maintains that atheists do not exist and that there are only believers and idolaters?

If I had a clear answer, I probably would have answered your first question more decisively. Basically, though, the people who think there are no atheists are the ones who believe that everyone is a potential convert. And I don't like to think of myself as somebody else's potential convert. My own religion is books, and to me the believers are the people who read, and the sad fact is that I'm just not very interested in people who don't read, unless they feel like converting to my religion. But things get tricky when I think about the fact that nonreaders are people, too, and that they have their own reasons for deciding not to be readers, and that maybe even this facetious distinction I've made, this division between readers and nonreaders, has something fundamentalist about it.

NEW YORK,
NOVEMBER 2004

SPIKE LEE

I No Longer Felt Anything in Church

I meet Spike Lee in the conference room on the tenth floor of the Tisch School of the Arts, at New York University. He's wearing an orange T-shirt and a Yankees cap. We have known each other a long time, and, ever since he's been teaching in the same department as I do, he has always found time periodically to ask me what's going on in Italian cinema. He agreed to talk about his relationship with religion as soon as I called him, but he insisted that the meeting take place immediately. "Tomorrow I'm starting work on an ad for the Knicks," he said, "and then I'm preparing for a film. Who knows when we'll speak again. The subject you're raising seems serious to me: it's better to get to it right away."

When I arrive at the conference room I find him studying a project entitled *Eventual Salvation*. He is leafing
through the manuscript with great interest, and when I ask
him jokingly, "Are you getting ready for the interview?" he
says, "It's a project submitted by a student. But if we want to
talk about spirituality, you must have observed that it's a
recurrent theme in my films."

*I would like to reflect on something more intimate, but let's
begin with your films. Which ones do you think touch on such
themes?*

Certainly *Malcolm X,* but also the documentary *4 Little
Girls.* And then who knows? Maybe the theme is present
but hidden in all the stories I've told.

Let's begin with Malcolm X.

I think that it's primarily a story of redemption, of a
transformation and a journey. In the film I think that this is
absolutely clear in the long sequence of Malcolm X's trip to
Mecca. The story I wanted to tell celebrates above all the
reawakening of a conscience and of a soul.

*In the final scene of the film, Malcolm X goes knowingly to the
place where he's going to be killed. He seems to be present at
Christ's ascent of Golgotha.*

You aren't the first to point that out to me, and I don't

deny it. In fact I'd like to emphasize that just before Malcolm X enters the place where he will be killed a colored woman goes up to him and says, "Jesus will pray for you."

Why did you cite Jesus?

Because Jesus' teachings are sublime, and I thought that the woman would console him by appealing to her own faith.

Why did you mention 4 Little Girls?

Primarily because the killing of the four colored girls happens in a church. The fact that a house of prayer is violated by a bomb makes the act even more abominable and blasphemous. In that period marked by segregation and racism, the churches represented first of all the heart of the African-American community, and the killing of four innocent children assumes a terrible symbolic significance. It is violence against the God they worshipped committed in the name of racial hatred. And it's violence on the part of persons who in some cases were certain that they worshipped their own god.

Does religion bring love or does it unleash hatred?

There are men who can unleash hatred by interpreting religions in their own way, just as there are religions, all too human, that can unleash hatred.

Can religion make the world a better place?

On the one hand you have the teachings or commandments; on the other, organized religion, and, in particular, those who represent it. Think of how the name of God has been abused in these years of religious conflicts. Think of how it has been invoked by those who have killed and urged others to kill. And think of a Protestant preacher like Pat Robertson, who said on television that he hoped for the assassination of President Chávez of Venezuela.

Let's go back to the cinema for a moment. What's the first film that comes to mind in which a strong spiritual yearning is present?

Of course, *On the Waterfront.*

It's a great, extremely controversial film.

The controversy and the antipathy with which a certain world sees it are due to Elia Kazan's position on McCarthyism. But they have nothing to do with the spiritual aspect of the film: *On the Waterfront* is essentially a story of redemption and salvation told in a remarkable way and with enormous passion. As a filmmaker I've always been overwhelmed by how great the directing is, and the acting, and the screenplay, by Budd Schulberg. But the film has especially a spiritual dimension—don't forget there's the crucial figure of the priest, played by Karl Malden. If I can mention some other examples I would say that I'm fascinated by films that are reworkings of ancient myths, like, for example, *Black Orpheus,* which reprises the myth of Orpheus and Eurydice.

Tell me about your religious upbringing.

My grandparents, on both sides, were very religious, but my parents were already much less so. I think I've continued this tendency.

What religion was it?

They were, or if you like we are, Southern Baptists. I think that the start of my progressive detachment coincided with the family's move to New York. My father was from Snow Hill, a tiny place in Alabama, and my mother is from Atlanta, which is where I was born, too. Sundays in church gave a rhythm and character to my childhood. I remember that the services were very long, and I couldn't sit still. And I remember especially that I didn't share the faith of the rest of the congregation, beyond the ritual, which today seems to me evocative and in some ways moving.

What does religion represent for you?

Something too human, which interprets and at times distorts spirituality.

What in your opinion is the difference between spirituality and religion?

I think that a superior being exists, but I don't believe in organized or institutionalized religion.

What is unconvincing to you about it?

Organized religion is managed by men.

Then who should manage it?

Let's say that men transform it into their own image and likeness.

The Bible teaches that God created man in his image and likeness.

That's exactly why the contrary frightens me. And yet the Bible has a precise and inescapable value for the believer.

Only for the believer?

Obviously there are infinite teachings that transcend faith, but I don't think it can be used as a point of reference on subjects of faith if the faith itself isn't there.

Do you ever feel the presence of God in daily life?

I feel a superior presence, which I don't know whether

to call God, when I'm with my wife and children. I believe strongly in the family. And I think that man is instinctively led to the good, and knows what is right and what is wrong.

How do you explain horrendous moments of history such as, for example, the Holocaust, or slavery?

Men are frail and imperfect and can commit terrible deeds. Tragedies and abominations like the ones you mentioned are part of human experience. Man can and knows how to reach the good, traveling a difficult path along which all his frailty emerges.

But do you think God is absent, distant, or mysterious?

I would like to have a precise answer, but I don't. I feel that a presence exists, but I don't know if I can call it God.

Many of those I've interviewed have reflected on Dostoyevsky's phrase "If God doesn't exist, everything is permitted."

I wonder what God Dostoyevsky is talking about. Everyone can construe it however he likes. It occurs to me that during the war Joe Louis said, "We're on God's side." You can't beat an appeal to the Omnipotent, and to convince your soldiers that God is on their side is an invincible weapon. But what do we know of what God can think if we don't even know if he exists? And am I mistaken or didn't the Germans, too, say "*Gott mit uns*"?

Do you think that a pure atheist can exist, or is it that a person who doesn't believe in God ends up believing in idols?
It's the doubt that torments every person who has closed the door to faith. I can answer that I have always had problems with respect to absolute positions. Maybe it's the sign of a road that I'm traveling on.

Do you think that in the case of an artist religion enriches him or weighs him down?
For centuries, the subject of art was religion. And many great artists were profoundly religious. But the point is the use that is made of it. Art is a tool for uplift.

Do you think it's possible to judge a work apart from its subject?
Yes, although I have to admit it regretfully.

What do you mean?
That, for example, Leni Riefenstahl was a great director who is still studied and imitated (think of *Star Wars*), but her subject was abominable. Think also of D. W. Griffith: no one doubts that *Birth of a Nation* is a milestone, but it's also

an exaltation of a violent and visceral racism, and the film was used as a recruiting tool for the K.K.K. Or even John Ford, a great filmmaker I can't love. In his films the only good Indian is a dead Indian.

NEW YORK,
SEPTEMBER 2005

DANIEL LIBESKIND

We Believe the Moment We See

I meet Daniel Libeskind on a hazy day at the end of June. From the wide windows of his studio, which faces Ground Zero, one can see the ocean as it meets New York Bay, and the small islands that welcomed millions of immigrants. Few parts of Manhattan communicate such an immediate sense of power, and the oppressiveness of the heat evident on the faces of the crowds outside contrasts with the relief of the air-conditioning, which immediately makes the studio a protected and privileged place. In the conference room where we are to meet, there are posters with Hebrew on them and a big plastic model that illustrates how the area destroyed by the attacks of September eleventh will be rebuilt.

When Libeskind arrives, he notes that I am admiring his work, and explains right away that this model is of the competition entry, and that there are more accurate models of the current version elsewhere in the studio. "As it happens, that's the case with this project, too," he says, with a mixture of enthusiasm and restraint, as he leads me toward another model. "It's a big residential center that I'm designing in Singapore. The architecture evolves the moment a project has been approved. And one never stops improving one's own ideas." He is a short man, cordial and with a ready smile, who says that he is "curious and willing" to speak about intimate subjects, and "absolutely honored" to appear in the company of figures he has always admired. "Shall we begin?" he says, catching me off guard. "Of course," I say, and try to maintain his rhythm by getting right to the point.

Do you believe in God?
I believe it's a question that always comes too late.

What do you mean?
That it's a retrospective question. Belief is an inescapable part of our daily experience. We believe the moment we see.

What is your idea of God?
I don't have a precise idea, nor do I believe that it's possible to have one.

Derek Walcott told me that his image of God is that of his child-hood: an old, bearded white man.

It's an evocative image, but personally I have never imagined the Heavenly Father like that. In fact, I don't even think it's possible to imagine him, but perhaps only to hear him.

Have you ever heard him?

Every day. I try to avoid the temptation to seek him only in moments of need.

So you hear him, or feel his presence, also in moments of certainty.

Absolutely. I believe that it's one of the very definitions of life. We didn't create ourselves alone.

St. Paul calls faith "the evidence of things unseen."

It's a perfect definition, to which I subscribe.

Do you consider yourself a man of faith?

I've never thought about it, nor have I ever asked myself the question, but I think I am.

Do you believe in a codified religion?

I would answer by saying that I'm Jewish. And that I come from a Hasidic tradition, in a world where my father and mother were the persons who rebelled against the dictates of religion. So I was brought up in a very secular way.

How did the Hasidic part of the family react?

As you might imagine. But this sort of diversity has always been present in the history of Judaism, which has also produced anarchists and revolutionaries.

Were you brought up to pray? To go to synagogue?

No, but I have to tell you that when I think of a person of great spirituality I think of my father: a man who said he didn't believe in God.

Obviously I wouldn't dream of questioning what you say about your father, yet don't you think that separating religiousness from codified religion opens the door to the risk of a generic and comfortable spirituality?

Certainly that's possible, and maybe even likely, but what seems most interesting to me is that one cannot escape spirituality. In my case, being Jewish I think implies an inescapable relationship with religion, but doesn't limit it. My personal journey has certainly been spiritual, but it hasn't followed the Orthodox itinerary.

Are there religious elements in your work?

Absolutely yes: I think that every project would be fallacious if it referred only to itself, or if it sought harmony only in itself. Even when we don't admit it, spirituality is a dimension of existence. We become aware of it at rare moments, when, for example, we are left speechless in the face of mystery or perfect beauty.

In your field are there architects in whom a religious background or yearning is evident?

The first name that comes to mind is obviously Antoni Gaudí. But in some ways it's too obvious. I've always been fascinated by the inescapable spirituality of a person considered a heretic, like Le Corbusier, or a mystic, like Mies van der Rohe, who read St. Thomas and St. Augustine and kept their books beside his bed. I would conclude by saying that there hasn't been a great architect who didn't have a strong element of spirituality.

Extending the question to art, is there an artist in whom you feel a strong sense of God?

I would turn the question around. I invite those who don't believe in God to listen to Bach. It's the first name that comes to mind, though certainly not the only one. He's not only a supreme musician but also a great architect. An artist who constructed great monuments that have no physicality.

What opportunity does religion offer?

The great religions are bound up in and at times identified with the history of civilization. It might seem self-evident, but I think every religion has the value of having placed God at the center of history. Man's temptation is to make God an extra. Personally I think we are also indebted to religions for the opportunity for doubt. Faith is a stimulus for religion, which otherwise would end up being rooted in absolute convictions.

What risks, on the other hand, do you think there are in religions?
The risks are terrible, and in recent years we have had continuous demonstrations of it. Those who take religion in a superficial or, worse, exploitative manner find in it the justification for acts that are anything but religious. And this attitude can generate conflict, violence, and suffering.

What are we asking when we ask ourselves whether God exists?
It's a question about freedom.

What do you mean?
Freedom means being free not only *from* something but *for* something. So the relationship to God doesn't depend on man. Otherwise freedom would be simply subjection to others.

NEW YORK,
JUNE 2005

DAVID LYNCH

_____

Good and Evil Are Within Us

I met David Lynch for the first time in 2001, at a screening organized at the Academy of Motion Pictures of the restored print of _8½_. I was struck by the passion that he brought to the event, and the emotion with which he spoke to me the next day of Federico Fellini. He had been introduced to Fellini in the eighties, by Isabella Rossellini, and he felt closely connected—a detail he was very proud of—by the fact of having been born on the same day, January 20.

I have to admit that I hadn't immediately thought of Lynch for this book. He's one of the most important and interesting American directors, and more than once has shown himself to be a genuine, original artist. Yet the presence of spirituality in his films seemed to me rare and iconographic, and at times I even had the sense that it was used as a pretext. In fact it was Isabella Rossellini who suggested that I interview him for this project, telling me about his meditation practice and the intensity with which he spoke about transcendent truths.

Meeting him when my book on contemporary American cinema was published, I asked him why there was never religion in his films, at least in its codified forms. His answer was: "I'm convinced that something, in fact a lot, exists that we don't know and of which we see only the semblances. I think that this element is present in my stories. I have no problem calling it spirituality or religion. Of course it's not codified, but this doesn't mean I'm expressing any judgment." Impelled by this memory, I decided to watch his films again before we met, but my initial puzzlement didn't change until I saw *The Straight Story*. The film seemed stylistically surprising and emotionally revealing. This story of an old man who decides to cross the United States on a tractor to be reconciled with his dying brother shows a grace and a yearning that I could only call religious. And as a result of that film, in particular the moving conclusion, in which the two men meet, I was able to analyze Lynch's entire artistic journey in a different light. Even the horror and the violence, a constant in his films, seemed to me the tortured complement of a search for harmony and a fear of the void. As soon as we begin to discuss these subjects, he asks me if I still think that *The Straight Story* is his best film.

I don't know. But I think that in some way it's the most revelatory, just because it's completely different from the others. At least in appearance.

But you know it's a film that I did for Canal Plus and that Disney then bought?

I know, but does that change anything? Even Bach wrote on commission, and there's an infinite number of artists who painted religious subjects they didn't believe in. But their works have lasted, and I don't think anyone can say what they actually thought and felt while they were executing them.

I know that when I was shooting the film I realized that it was different from my others.

Do you mean that you didn't identify with what you were shooting?

I'm not saying that, and in fact I made an effort to respect the sentiments of the screenplay, by John Roach, on which my longtime collaborator Mary Sweeney worked as well.

Before getting to your personal relationship with faith, I want to ask you why your films emphasize mystery, the paranormal, and the absurd.

I could confine myself to saying that I'm fascinated by all these elements, but also I don't think anyone can assume for himself the right to say what's absurd and what's logical, what's normal and what's paranormal. And we could talk for a long time about the concept of mystery: the human mind works on intuition, and so it is able to intuit abstraction, too. Cinema is the language of images in motion, so it forces the author to express these abstractions in gestures and actions. As an artist I'm fascinated by every creation that originates in this opposition.

What's surprising in The Straight Story *is the cathartic conclusion—I would even venture to call it redemptive.*

The film has an extremely linear style, and yet it obeys the very principle that I was trying to express: the moment the performance begins, an illusion is created, and the degree of abstraction increases. I think that redemption, a potential innate in every human being, is part of this mystery.

From the way you speak it seems that the spiritual is very present in your life.

Absolutely, but you have to understand the meaning of the term *spiritual*.

Let's get to the direct question: do you believe in God?

I think that a divine being exists who is omnipotent and eternal.

How do you picture him?

I don't imagine him apart from the characteristics I've just mentioned.

What do you think of organized religions?

I respect them, as I respect those who follow their teachings, but I don't belong to one.

Tell me about your religious education.

I was brought up as a Presbyterian, and I went to church until I was fourteen. Then I politely asked my parents for permission to do without it. I think I can say that since then I've felt what I later elaborated with greater clarity—that is, that each of us has within the potential for revelation, and for perceiving the existence of the divine.

What memories do you have of the God you prayed to in those years?

I recall a sensation of happiness. But many of those elements are still present in my convictions, like the idea of God the compassionate father. And I often think of the idea of the Kingdom of Heaven.

You don't feel the need for a church that acts as a bond between you and this omnipotent being?

No. But that doesn't mean that I'm against churches. Each of us follows his own path.

Could one say that inside you remained a Protestant?

You can certainly say it, but I don't feel that I am one. Protestantism is also a church.

In your films evil is absolute, and good is the sign of a purity that borders on holiness. Doesn't that seem a Manichaean formulation?

The first answer that occurs to me is that it's uniquely the way I express myself artistically. But I want to add that I don't think that something exists that's in itself bad or good; it's our way of seeing it that renders it such.

Do you mean that neither good nor evil exists?

What I mean is that they are within us, and come from there.

Are there films by other directors that you would say have strong spiritual elements?

The list would be endless. But I have to confess that many of the films that strike me that way wouldn't be among the usual choices.

What do you mean?

That the classic responses would include artists who are certainly great, like Buñuel, Dreyer, or Fellini, while for me films like Robert Benton's *Places in the Heart* and Harold Ramis's *Groundhog Day* come to mind. I find that in both there is a breath of the divine as strong as that in the works that are usually celebrated. And the ending of *Places in the Heart* has always seemed to me intensely moving, when all the characters find themselves in church.

In recent years you have devoted a lot of energy and passion to transcendental meditation.

It's a personal way of trying to have a conversation with the divinity. But I must correct you: I've been practicing transcendental meditation for more than thirty years. What's new is that I've recently started a project with my foundation to disseminate this practice as widely as possible.

The name you chose is Foundation for Consciousness-Based Education and World Peace. Doesn't it seem a little generic?

Not at all. Ambitious, maybe, but I don't consider that a flaw. Rather, it's something that helps me pursue my purpose.

Is it true that one of the people who led you to transcendental meditation was Maharishi Mahesh Yogi, who in the seventies was the Beatles' spiritual guru?

It's true: I met him through my sister. I think he's a holy man, and I owe to him the discovery that the possibility for happiness dwells within us.

What about that is different from St. Augustine's "Noli foras ire, in te ipsum redi, in interiore homine habitat veritas" ("Go not about, retire within: Truth dwells in the inner man")?

Transcendental meditation is a mental technique that I practice twice a day; it allows each human being to dive into his own ego and reach pure consciousness and pure happiness. In St. Augustine, on the other hand, it's all closely tied to Christian revelation. Having said that, I think that every human being is destined to happiness, that every form of negativity is like the darkness, which disappears as soon as you light the light of peace, piety, and unity.

I know that you consider it an exception, but the film that clearly expresses what you're saying is The Straight Story.

Let's say that I would never have agreed to direct it if I hadn't felt something that touched me closely.

Have you ever tried to communicate in your films what you've learned from Maharishi Mahesh Yogi?

It's inevitable that an artist expresses what he believes in and what he feels within himself. But as you know I love abstraction, and so I don't think I've ever done it consciously. I'm afraid of propaganda, and I go along with the old Hollywood saying that if you have to send a message, use a telegram.

NEW YORK,
JANUARY 2006

TONI MORRISON

———

The Search Is More Important
Than the Conclusion

oni Morrison was born seventy-three years ago in
Lorain, a small city in Ohio, with the name Chloe
Anthony Wofford. It was she who chose the nickname Toni,
when she got tired of the way her baptismal name kept getting mangled. She was the first black woman (and eighth
woman overall) to be awarded the Nobel Prize in Literature
("In novels characterized by a visionary force and poetic
import, she gives life to an essential aspect of American reality."), and she received the Pulitzer Prize in 1988 for her
novel *Beloved*. She was an esteemed editor at Random
House for twenty years and Robert F. Goheen Professor of
Humanities at Princeton University for eighteen years.

She asks me to meet her in her apartment in New York,

in a building that once housed the city's police headquarters. She is a woman of majestic bearing and a gaze that makes one uneasy; she wears her long gray hair in braids, and her voice reveals a faint cadence of the South, where her parents were from originally. She is immediately aware of my amazement at the strange architecture of the building, which still displays the flags and the decor of its former occupation, but she urges me to admire its grandeur and consider how badly used the spaces were until now. "If we are to talk about our relationship with God, I suppose we should look for it in everything," she says jokingly before asking me to choose a restaurant where we can reflect at leisure on a subject that she would never have imagined discussing publicly.

These days, politicians and institutions talk about God constantly.

I think what they're doing is simply exploitative, if not blasphemous. The situation this president has got us into is desperate, and I'm terrified when I hear him speak of his God. Phrases are attributed to him like "I will never negotiate with myself," but negotiating with oneself is what is normally called thinking. His religious absolutism is stupefying. I can't understand with what moral authority he refers to the Heavenly Father and then calls himself a war president. To me, it seems he bases his power on fear.

Tell me about your attitude toward God. Do you believe in him?

I believe in an intelligence interested in what exists and respectful of what is created.

How does this definition differ from the God of religions?

In the fact that every religion ends by defining and hence reducing him. My idea of God is that of an infinite growing that discourages definitions but not knowledge. I believe in an intellectual experience that intensifies our perceptions and distances us from an egocentric and predatory life, from ignorance and from the limits of personal satisfactions. The greater our knowledge, the greater God becomes. Even the Bible, this marvelous book written by extraordinary visionaries, is small and reductive with respect to the greatness of God.

You speak of a definition that creates a limit. Yet faith does not claim to define.

That's true, but I'm also thinking of the fact that the search is always more important than the conclusion, and at times the conclusion is in the journey.

Tell me about your inner religious journey.

I had a Catholic education, even though my mother, who was very religious, was Protestant. As a child I was fascinated by the rituals of Catholicism, and I was strongly influenced by a cousin who was a fervent Catholic.

When did your relationship with Catholicism end?

I don't know how to explain it. It might surprise you to
know that I had a moment of crisis on the occasion of Vatican II. At the time I had the impression that it was a superficial change, and I suffered greatly from the abolition
of Latin, which I saw as the unifying and universal language of the Church. But I still find the revolution of love
that replaced the idea of justice astonishing. It's something
extremely modern, and perhaps eternal, which someone
brought to humanity.

For those who believe, that "someone" is the son of God.

If he isn't that, we are speaking certainly of a genius.
It's love that distinguishes us from the animals. And in this
revolution attention to the weakest and smallest becomes
central.

*You speak of the Christian revolution with emotion, and yet
today you believe in an intelligent entity.*

I don't believe in a God the father: even that seems to me
a limitation, not to say a simplification. And I challenge the
image of God as a protective father: if I try to imagine
his essence, and think, for example, of the infiniteness of
time, I get lost in a mixture of dismay and excitement. I
sense the order and harmony that suggest an intelligence,

and I discover, with a slight shiver, that my own language becomes evangelical.

Derek Walcott talked about this problem, with respect to De Chirico's The Nostalgia of the Infinite, *at the Museum of Modern Art.*

It's the perfect dilemma: the greatest and most eternal. We feel ourselves unique, and in many ways we are, but we also feel that we belong to something greater, about which we can only feel nostalgia.

Do you think that those who believe are deluded?

No, on the contrary: I feel the greatest respect for them, and certainly I am not the one to judge. Yet I think that the mind always tries to protect itself, and that the attitude of a person who finds a system to believe in is very human. The tendency to humanize the divinity has always amused me: I think of men who exalt the warrior aspect or the Catholic nuns who called themselves brides of Christ. Or those who identify him with doctor, soldier, husband: they are rather obvious examples of human needs.

Your intellectual approach seems to originate in the "Intellego ut credam" *("I understand in order that I may believe").*

I want to stop on the term *Intellego,* because I know that

there always exists a yearning for God. All the mind can do is learn, and the moment when the mind stops coincides with death.

What does death mean to you?

In moments of depression I see it as a liberation, but normally it represents something inconceivable: we live in the paradox of not accepting the most obvious and inevitable of our conditions.

The subject of your university thesis was death, and, in particular, suicide in Faulkner and Woolf.

Death is an unacceptable fact that we must nevertheless confront: I chose that subject in order to consider the fact that in *Absalom, Absalom!* the American Faulkner describes suicide as an act of weakness, whereas in *Mrs. Dalloway* the English Woolf transforms it into a heroic act of freedom.

Your books have religious references even in the titles.

It's true, but I must tell you that both *Song of Solomon* and *Paradise* are titles suggested by the editor. Consider that the original title of the latter book, in which all the characters are believers, was *War*. *Beloved* is taken from a quotation in St. Paul's letter to the Corinthians, but it's also a way of relating to something profoundly intimate and essential.

One of your recurring themes is slavery. Do you think of it only as a physical condition?

No, absolutely not. The abomination of a human being put in chains is one of the greatest tragedies of humanity, but I know of course that psychological and ideological slaveries also exist.

Do you think that religion is present in modern art?

Less than one might imagine, and often it's used for commercial purposes. Think, for example, of those pretentious bad films in which angels appear as dei ex machina, or of figurative artists who use religious iconography with the sole purpose of creating a scandal. It's not serious—it's supermarket religion, a spiritual Disneyland of false fear and pleasure.

But in art is religion a limitation or an opportunity?

I think it's neutral. There are writers and poets who don't believe and have made marvelous works with religious subjects.

What writers who have treated religious subjects do you most admire?

Joyce, in particular the youthful works, and Flannery O'Connor, a great artist who hasn't received the attention she deserves. They are the writers who come immediately to mind, but let's not forget the Russians: Dostoyevsky, Tolstoy, and even Chekhov never left the Heavenly Father in peace.

NEW YORK,
FEBRUARY 2004

GRACE PALEY

Death Is the End of Everything

Grace Paley was born in the Bronx in 1922 into a Jewish family that had fled to America from czarist Russia. She considers herself American, but she often wonders what her life would have been if Isaac and Mary, as her parents were called here, had remained in the land of their forebears. She has lived for many years in Vermont, in the town of Thetford, but she still has an apartment in Greenwich Village, and she welcomes me there as if I were a dear friend. This is due entirely to her sociability, because we had met only once before, and that interview was never published. She insists that I call her Grace, and she is curious about the fact that I want to talk about her relationship with religion.

While she prepares green tea she asks how I came to get involved in a subject like this.

I think it's the most important subject of our time. Rather, the most important of all times.

Are you serious?

Of course—and I have to assume that it's not for you.

I would say that our relationship with the soul is an eternal theme.

Do you believe in God?

No. But I've always had a profound interest in the Bible.

From what point of view?

From a historical and literary point of view. I have no hesitation in calling it the book of books, but for me it has no religious value. I think it's a marvelous historical book, with great moments of poetry, which tells the story of a people that is defining itself.

What are you referring to when you say poetry?

For example, the Psalms of David. The fact that this great poet was also a warrior king has always been both disturbing and moving to me.

Why did you mention only the Old Testament?

Because I don't love the New Testament as much.

Why not?

It seems to me that what has been up to that point a marvelous journey of definition and self-definition becomes propagandistic.

What do you mean?

Well, maybe I used a strong and reductive word: let's say that it becomes purely religious, and in terms of my approach not interesting.

Christ speaks to the Jews and the Gentiles.

I know, and I'm always touched by Christ's words. I have greater problems with Paul: it's with him that the new religion becomes institutionalized, and I think that this was a mistake.

Do you believe in the historical figure of Christ?

Yes, of course, and I think he was one of the greatest and most profound thinkers in history. To deny that would be an act of ignorance.

Tell me about your religious education.

There is very little to tell: my parents were both atheists, and when they fled Russia they were against the rabbis no less than they were against the czar.

There was no one in your family who talked to you about religion, or gave you any religious education?

The only person who had some faint religious feelings was my grandmother Natasha. As long as she was alive she lived with us, and she was the only one with whom every so often I would talk about the soul. I can say the same with regard to my siblings: none of us ever believed in God.

What do you feel when you meet a believer?

I feel ambivalent: I respect his thinking and his belief, but at the same time I think he's deluded. This doesn't mean that it doesn't interest me to start a discussion: I am always curious about ideas, especially those very different from my own.

What do you think when you hear or read the words of a religious leader?

It depends. I'm sure that there are some of absolutely good faith whom I wouldn't hesitate to call holy men. But I don't think this opinion can be extended to all.

Do you think there is life after death?

Obviously no. And an eighty-three-year-old is telling you this, aware that she doesn't have much longer to live. The moment I take my last breath everything will end. Bye-bye—in fact, farewell.

And what are your thoughts about that?
That it's sad, but life is wonderful.

Has it never happened to you that in the presence of something particularly beautiful or overwhelming you felt the existence of something superior?
I've felt the existence of mystery. This yes, I don't deny it. Nor would I deny that inexplicable things happen repeatedly, and even miracles. But I don't connect these events to an omnipotent and omniscient presence.

Have you never felt nostalgia for religion, which is such an important element of your tradition?
No, but I have to confess that in the past ten years I've begun to go to synagogue again.

It seems to me that this refutes everything you've told me up to now.
I must make a second confession: the reason I go to synagogue is not religious. Ever since I went to live in Vermont,

with my second husband, Robert Nichols, I've felt the need to find my community. I was born and grew up in the Bronx in a completely Jewish neighborhood, and today I find myself in a rural area that's almost entirely Christian. The meeting place is the synagogue.

But doesn't it seem to you that you're exploiting religion for a need of another type?

Maybe, but I also know that my tradition is one with religion, and who knows, maybe I even feel a call. Recently I've fallen into heated discussions with the rabbi after the service . . . even though for me what happens before my eyes in the temple is little more than a theater performance.

Is your husband religious?

He is an Episcopalian. But I wouldn't say that he's a very observant person. Nor was my first husband, a Jew. May I ask you a question, at this point?

Of course.

Why did you say that our relationship with religion is important at this moment in particular?

I was referring to what is happening in the world. For example, do you think that religion is an opportunity for peace or for war?

It can be both, and history has shown us this repeatedly. I

think that in conflicts with a religious dimension war is inevitable if one doesn't give up something.

But now I want to ask you a second question.

Please.
Do you believe?

I am Catholic, Apostolic, Roman.
And what is there for you after death?

The true life.
And what is the life that we're living at this moment?

A passage and a gift.
Now, you see, this is an idea that interests me, because it's very different from what I believe in. Do you think you're happier than I am?

This I don't know, but I know that St. Paul, whom you are not fond of, says: "Happiness is in your hearts." Now let me assume my role again.
Provided you are willing to give it up again.

I promise. I'd like to submit to you a quotation that I asked many of my interview subjects to comment on. It is Dostoyevsky's "If God doesn't exist, then everything is permitted."

I've never believed it. It seems to me that it diminishes humanity and man's inner conscience. The world has committed monstrosities despite believing in God and following (or at least believing it is following) his teachings. What has to do with the life of humanity has nothing to do with the possible existence of the Omnipotent. And I say this with the knowledge that the mystery endures—or, if you like, dominates.

Do you think then that faith is only an illusion?

I think it can also be a useful instrument—for improving the world, for example. Do you feel that you are better as a result of your faith?

I would feel useless without it. And even more useless without charity.

I'm ahead of you. I know you're quoting the hymn to charity—it's a passage from Paul. And I would add, on charity I am in total agreement. One of the most beautiful, gratifying, and enriching experiences of my life was my involvement with the Catholic Worker Movement. One can say what one likes about faith, but what I saw done by its members daily and by all who were the heirs of Dorothy Day is simply marvelous: an extraordinary lesson for us all on what it means to love and to work to make the world a better place with determination and a spirit of service. It was an experience that formed my social, political, and even artistic conscience.

What do you mean when you speak of the formation of an artistic conscience?

I refer to something that I can't define clearly, but that is certainly present. I wonder, for example, how an atheist like me, who at most conceives the existence of mystery, has written some poems about God.

Are you saying that there is something not definitive in your belief? Or, rather, in your lack of belief?

It would be serious if that were not the case. Absolute positions frighten me. But I don't feel what you believers call grace. I feel, rather, part of the great and marvelous mystery of existence, and I wonder what we'll be in a million years. Today I see that there is so much life that we want to destroy.

Are there writers you admire in whom the religious element is dominant?

How can one not admire Dante? But I think that even he, like all artists who believe in God, had his moments of doubt.

NEW YORK,
OCTOBER 2005

SALMAN RUSHDIE

I Believe in a Mortal Soul

By pure coincidence, I met Salman Rushdie on April 8, 2005, the day of Pope John Paul II's funeral. When I arrived at our meeting, my mind was filled with images of the exultant crowd—filled with the joy that only believers feel at the moment of death—against the extraordinary backdrop of St. Peter's Square: Michelangelo's cupola, Bernini's colonnade, the dazzling red of the cardinals, and the modest black of the powerful of the world—kings, queens, presidents, and prime ministers. It was a luminous April day in New York, but, even as I was about to meet a writer who had been condemned to death on the charge of having insulted Islam, I couldn't help thinking of those images of the Vatican, and in particular of the representatives of all the other religions around the plain cypress bier, on which a Gospel had been placed, its pages ruffling in the wind. Around this bier sworn enemies shook hands in a sign of peace; could this be taken as a symbol of how the world might be? Rome seemed to me the *caput mundi,* the head of the world, as it had not been for hundreds, perhaps thousands of years.

The presence of the flags and those people of so many different religions made me reflect on the different faces we attribute to God. For example, Rabbi Elio Toaff, the former chief rabbi of Rome, mentioned affectionately by the Pope in his will—to whom was the rabbi praying? How did he imagine the Omnipotent in praying for his dead friend, the high priest of another religion? And to whom, exactly, were the millions of faithful turning on that day of mourning and exultation? Were they all really believers? Or for many was it simply a matter of emotion—intense certainly, but destined to cool, or to be choked by thorns, as the parable of the sower recounts?

Rushdie must have thought I was a real oddball when, after we had been introduced by his agent, I said nothing for quite some time. In fact I was still thinking of the very different effect that such a critical event can have on people who have made widely divergent choices. The sight of the square filled with banners and mourners seemed to make atheism inconceivable, and yet, I thought, even Christ endured moments of rebellion or indifference on the part of his followers. Maybe the merit of faith is precisely this, I thought, but the problem of grace stayed with me. How is it that one becomes a believer? What happens? And how is it that one chooses instead not to believe? What is it that doesn't click? What is it that gives a finite and material vision of the world? Is it possible to be truly happy when one comes to a conclusion like that? Doesn't life become a hell?

And if, on the other hand, faith is an illusion, a precautionary consolation before the great void? In these conversations concerning the idea of God what struck me most intensely was something a nonbeliever said, quoting a passage from St. Paul: "Faith is the evidence of things unseen." It seems a paradox, and perhaps it is. But what else is faith?

After a few minutes, during which my thoughts wandered as I continued to stare at him, Rushdie gave a legitimate sign of impatience and decided to start in: "From what we've seen on television today the weather is much nicer here than in Rome. That's pretty rare."

Did you watch the funeral?
Part of it. But who didn't?

What was your impression?

The ceremony was extraordinarily evocative, but I don't think I'm the right person to give a better answer.

What do you mean?

That I saw a lot of emotion, a lot of joy, but as far as I'm concerned the Pope, who certainly had a rich and meaningful life, is dead forever. Like everyone.

When did you stop believing in God?

I don't think I ever believed.

Tell me about your religious education.

I'm from a Muslim family. My father was a great religious scholar, but he wasn't a believer. My mother, on the other hand, was mildly observant. But in my family there is a genuine spiritual tradition. My grandfather was extremely religious, and at the same time open and tolerant like few people I've met in my life. I still remember, with emotion, many discussions of religion, and the affection and respect with which he tried to understand why I didn't believe. He encouraged me to talk about it, wanting, humbly, in his turn to understand. My grandfather—in particular, his approach to religion—was fundamentally important in my writing and in my entire existence.

At school, what sort of religious education did you have?

I went to a school called the English Mission School, with students from every part of the world. I was brought up to pray, but I recall that I repeated the prayers without much understanding of what they said.

In the course of a conversation I had for the draft of this book, Derek Walcott, who says he is a believer, told me that the image he has of God is still that of an old, white man with a beard.

If I have to think of an image, that's the one I have, too, and I can't get free of it, but the difference is that I'm not a believer.

You say that you never believed. But was there a moment of crisis or rethinking?

Reflection, of course, is continuous, but I wouldn't use the word *crisis.* Unfortunately I can't get over a tragic fact that is intimately bound up with religion.

Which is?

The blood that's shed in the name of God. And obviously I mean every religion. Don't forget that I was born in 1947, the year of the massacres between Hindus and Muslims and the separation of India and Pakistan.

You don't think that this is one of the many tragic events to be attributed to men who exploit, betray, and blaspheme the will of God?

When you don't believe, it's difficult to separate the two things, and little remains.

Do you think that religion represents something negative?

I think it's dangerous when it is strikingly opposed to reason: think of the case of Terri Schiavo, the woman in a coma whose case recently set off a revival of the religious right. I think that in reality this poor woman had been dead for fifteen years, from the moment she fell into a coma. We all knew that there was no real possibility that she would return to normal life.

Religion teaches us to defend life to the last breath.

The fact is, I think she was already dead.

There are instances of people who have come out of a coma, and I'm not suggesting miracles.

It doesn't seem to me that in this case there was a single doctor who contemplated such an eventuality. It was a situation where religion, or at least the use that was made of it by some, in my opinion had a negative value.

Religion follows paths different from reason.

That's an element that reinforces my distance.

Many of your characters are religious or have a religious background.

It would be ridiculous if that were not the case, especially in novels more directly tied to my culture. But this fact has to do with my journey as an artist, and is obviously an attempt to understand a fundamental element.

You have often said that your cultural education took place at the movies.

It's true, and in particular thanks to Italian movies.

Movies in which the spiritual element is very present.

It's true but not always. I still have enormous love for Fellini, De Sica, and Rossellini, in whom religion is present, and Visconti, where it seems to me much less visible. I admit that recently I've had some problems with a director I loved in the past, Antonioni. I have the impression that existential angst hasn't aged well, and while I could watch *La Dolce Vita* or *The Bicycle Thief* every night, I would be a little afraid of seeing a film like *L'Avventura*. Although I must say that I recently saw *The Passenger* and it still seems to me very effective and moving.

Are there writers who have confronted religious subjects whom you admire?

Many, but the first who comes to mind is Saul Bellow,

whose intimate, unbreakable bond with religion and Jewish philosophy hasn't been sufficiently analyzed.

When I interviewed him for this book, he told me that he believes in God, but that he doesn't want to bug him.

That seems to me a pure Bellovian remark, which confirms what I've just said. But I also want to mention Czeslaw Milosz, a marvelous poet; his poetry is great because of the sense of spirituality that comes from his religion. Both Bellow and Milosz are constantly examining the soul.

Do you believe in the soul?

I believe that something mysterious and incomprehensible exists, but it's not transcendent or supernatural. So I use the word *soul* because there isn't a more efficacious or secular one. In other words, I believe in a mortal soul.

NEW YORK,
APRIL 2005

ARTHUR SCHLESINGER, JR.

I Am an Agnostic

The windows of Arthur Schlesinger, Jr.'s apartment are covered with ice as a result of the worst cold spell to hit America in recent decades, and our discussion of his personal relationship with religion takes place in an environment that seems harsh outside and cozy inside. He doesn't seem especially interested in knowing who else agreed to be interviewed, but he is curious about a subject "that it's impossible to escape." After checking the latest international political news on TV, he says, "In the past I would never have expected that I would be asked to talk about a subject like this, but I realize that what at times seems to us old-fashioned is in reality eternal, and that every political choice originates in inner convictions."

Do you think it's right for a government to have a religious inspiration?

It depends on what you mean by inspiration. I have a lay and secular approach, and personally I would find myself very uneasy in a country where religion had a central role. Faith is an intimate thing and should remain that way. This obviously doesn't mean that I don't believe in total freedom of worship. We have seen too many dictatorships in which religion was outlawed. In many of those cases religion ended up being identified with freedom.

Do you think that in America a religious inspiration is unavoidable?

I would say it's inevitable. In recent years religion has gained a central role, I don't know with how much good faith on the part of those who govern us. I believe in absolute separation of church and state, and I am among those who agree, for instance, with the recent choices made by President Chirac. A modern country has to guarantee religious freedom, but, just to take an example that's been in the news, ban the head scarf worn by Muslim women.

What is the boundary between religious inspiration and fundamentalism?

The fundamentalists believe in a literal interpretation of their book of worship. This is a phenomenon that has had less disruptive characteristics in the United States than in other countries, and certainly less violent. It's enough to think of Muslim or Hindu fundamentalism. Yet we've had our share of horrors and discrimination. The Protestant fanaticism of the towns of the so-called Bible Belt is characterized by both anti-Semitic and anti-Catholic attitudes. I remember personally the hostility toward John F. Kennedy, who was reprising what had happened in 1928 with Al Smith, the first Catholic Democratic presidential candidate, who was defeated by Hoover.

Do you think that the situation has changed?

I remember that in my youth the Christian fundamentalists were considered little more than an obscure sect. Today they have formed a close alliance with the Catholic right and the Jewish right. From a political point of view it is estimated that this alliance controls around 40 percent of the vote, and I don't hesitate to say that I am both concerned and dismayed.

In his 2005 State of the Union address, President Bush made constant references to religion, and also proposed easing the tax burden of religious organizations that do charitable works.

He doesn't make any more references to God than his predecessors did, but, because of the support Bush has received from evangelical groups, those references particularly stand out. As for the tax breaks, those who do charitable works are obviously doing something deserving, but the need to emphasize it in a speech like that is striking.

There are those who paint America as a country that oscillates between Puritanism and consumerism.

One should never confuse the corruption of a reality with the true essence of that same reality. I would reject the propagandistic formulation, but I don't want to conceal from myself the risk.

Do you think that the United States is a country where religious freedom has been realized or has the Calvinist influence been dominant?

The freedom of worship that we enjoy in the United States has up to now been a model, and the tragic conflicts that we are living through are a result of this characteristic. That being said, one cannot deny the effect of Protestant culture, and in particular of Calvinism, which has influenced politics, society, and capitalism.

Can you give me an example of a politician who benefited from his religious inspiration?

If it's combined with a lay approach, religious inspiration can't help having a positive effect. There is no American president who has not made his own beliefs evident, and who the Sunday before the election does not make a show of going to pray with the family. I would answer with a remark of Lincoln's: "The Almighty has his own purposes."

Give me a negative example.

Even in this case I am reluctant to name names. I can tell you that there is nothing more dangerous than a person in politics who is certain that he is acting in the name of God. I've always liked the definition of a fanatic given by Mr. Dooley, the character invented by Finley Peter Dunne: "A man that does what he thinks th' Lord wud do if He knew th' facts iv th' case."

You worked with Kennedy, who caused a sensation just by the fact of being the first Catholic president.

I must say that I never saw anything in his public acts that gave evidence of his belief. From this point of view we were similar, and kept religion in the personal sphere.

So, Mr. Schlesinger, do you believe in God?
No.

How would you define yourself from a religious point of view?
An agnostic.

Tell me about your religious education.

I grew up in a Congregationalist family, which converted to Unitarianism when we moved to Cambridge. I began not to believe in the existence of God when I was in high school.

What was the turning point?

I read a book that struck me irrevocably: *An Agnostic's Apology* by Leslie Stephen. Stephen is a thinker who is not studied today as he should be—at most, he is known for being the father of Virginia Woolf—but the influence he had on many people of my generation is enormous, in particular for that book and for the term *agnostic*. The word was coined some years earlier by Thomas Huxley, but it was Stephen who made it a fundamental reference in the culture and in the field of personal choices.

In The Brothers Karamazov, *Ivan says, with dismay, "If God doesn't exist, everything is permitted."*

It's one of the passages of Dostoyevsky that have always disturbed me, and that lead me inevitably to reflect on the mysteries of existence and on the presence of good and evil. However, I would like to dissent: man has been able to give himself laws and rules for a civilized society. He has been able to be tolerant and to love. There are those who don't want to believe that the absence of God leads inevitably to tragedy, and we can't forget that the history of man has taught us that in the name of God an infinite number of errors and horrors have been committed.

But those are instances of fanaticism, a betrayal of what for believers God communicated to man by revealing himself. Instead, the horrors of a world without God seem to originate, as Dostoyevsky maintains, in the fact of his absence.

It's certainly something we should reflect on as we struggle to assert the rules of civilization and tolerance that man is capable of providing by himself.

A believer could say that those rules and that capacity to love reflect the spark of the divine that is in every human being.

An agnostic like me knows that he has these principles and this tension in himself, and the duty to follow them.

How does an agnostic like you face death?

Paradise can't exist without an inferno. But I don't believe in either one. I believe that death is simply the end.

NEW YORK,
JANUARY 2005

MARTIN SCORSESE

God Is Not a Torturer

I met Martin Scorsese for the first time in 1985, as he was getting ready to shoot *After Hours.* It was a few months after the release of *The King of Comedy,* one of my favorites among his films, and I had requested an interview for the newspaper I wrote for at that time. To anyone who loved cinema, Scorsese was a legend. I had at least three reasons to admire unconditionally what he was doing in cinema and for cinema. First, he directed *Raging Bull,* the best film ever made about boxing (among my weaknesses is an unhealthy fascination with that sport). Second, he reveals in his films a love for New York City equal only to that of Woody Allen. Third, he had begun to fight for the reappraisal and preservation of films, and had an amazing collection of films himself. Only later did I begin to appreciate in his films the inescapable presence of a Catholic faith experienced in a manner both intimate and controversial, but even by the end of that meeting I had begun to document the personal journey of a director who as a child had been an altar boy and had later declared that for an adolescent in Little Italy the only paths available seemed to be those of the gangster and the priest.

Scorsese's office at the time was in an old building just off Times Square. I had arrived very early for the appointment, and of that long wait I recall the huge original posters for old films that covered the walls, Paul Schrader wandering in the corridors with a screenplay under his arm, and the sudden arrival of Scorsese himself, accompanied by a poodle. I was very excited, and when I was admitted to his office I nervously started off by saying that I, too, was a film collector and already had eight hundred titles in my archive. Scorsese told me that he had nine thousand, and when he began explaining the difficulty of preserving film I didn't dare to tell him that my collection was made up of videocassettes. But what won me over immediately was that he took me seriously, treating as an equal an unknown young man who wanted to interview him. I have never met anyone who spoke so rapidly, but his ever-present sense of irony and the naturalness with which he tried repeatedly to involve me in his passion for his favorite films (*The Wild Bunch, Paisan, 8½* . . . the list is infinite) revealed a person different from what I had imagined. In the Scorsese I had before me there was nothing to suggest the violence he expressed in his films, and yet it was evident that the torments, the neuroses, and the explosiveness of his characters reflected something he felt deeply, as did the yearning for redemption and the search—dramatic, and often thrown off course—for purity.

I've never had the chance to visit him on the set, but over the years, thanks to some mutual friends, a relationship developed between us that has enabled me to discover two fundamental elements of his character: a surprising intellectual humility and an exquisite generosity. I had confirmation of this when Scorsese, upon discovering that delaying the interview might delay the book's publication date, decided to go ahead with it even though he had a fever. Our conversation began after he apologized profusely for his hoarse voice.

How important is your Catholic upbringing in your films?

Catholicism has been extraordinarily important in my life, and I would say that my films would be inconceivable without the presence of religion. Because I developed asthma when I was three, my childhood was marked by solitude and isolation. Ever since, my reference points have been the family, the church, and then the cinema. Outside there were also the streets, with all their temptations and possibilities of ruin, and in each of these cardinal points I saw the oscillation between the sacred and the profane.

I read a statement of yours: "I'm a lapsed Catholic. But I am Roman Catholic—there's no way out of it." What do you mean?

Maybe *lapsed* is too strong a term, and then I don't know who can call himself both lapsed and Catholic. But what I meant is that I am not strictly orthodox, and that in many ways I feel I haven't respected the requirements of the Christian message. And yet I think that my Catholicism is part of my innermost self, and I'm sure it will always be that way.

Do you believe in God?

I don't think I can give a precise answer. I think that my faith in God lies in my constant searching. But certainly I call myself a Catholic.

How can you be a Catholic and not be sure if you believe in God?

I didn't say that. What I'm trying to explain is that I

distrust definitions, and I think there are questions that I personally find it difficult to respond to directly.

For a Catholic, God is made flesh, is born of a virgin, and saves the world.

I would answer that everything you've said is part of my culture, of what I try to express in my films, and so of my being.

Were your parents observant?

Religion played an important role in their life, but as far as I was concerned they weren't especially strict. Yet at home the iconography was very visible. My grandmother had a portrait of the Sacred Heart in her room, and a niche where there was a Virgin treading on the serpent. I also remember a large crucifix, on which she placed the blessed palms of Palm Sunday.

What made you move toward religion?

Apart from the iconography, which is so powerful and evocative, the dramaturgical aspect of Mass and the religious services. But obviously I felt something more profound, beginning with the idea of suffering and redemption, which obsessed me, and which I saw in both the intimacy and the externality of Catholicism. Maybe it's no coincidence that in those years I was a fan of film noir, in which the same elements clash.

What do you remember of the period when you were an altar boy?

The ritual and the liturgical markers of the year, elements that influenced me profoundly from both the dramaturgical and the existential point of view. I remember the excitement of Palm Sunday, but also the ritual of the washing of the feet and Holy Friday. And I remember meeting a young priest named Francis Principe, with whom I shared a passion for movies. He had been ordained in 1952, when I was only ten, and I saw in him a different possibility, in fact opposite to what the streets of Little Italy offered. Father Principe was an idealist, and he represented a mentor and a model. He was Italian-American, like me, and I owe to his teaching my earliest thoughts on the concept of grace and redemption. I often assisted him as an altar boy at funerals, and I remember fondly now how sorry he was when I arrived late for evening Mass, and the disappointment he felt whenever I got in trouble.

Growing up Catholic in Little Italy, one was often forced to confront violence.

I would say that this is valid not only for Little Italy. But I recall details and rituals of those streets that bordered on paganism. I remember seeing a Puerto Rican boy kiss his knife during a street fight, an image I've often adopted in my movies.

I found an interview with Gene Siskel in 1988 in which you said, "I took the Gospel very seriously. I wondered then and I still wonder whether I should quit everything and help the poor. But I wasn't, and I'm still not, strong enough."

There is little to add, except that the obligation to do good is something that every person who has a conscience should feel. As you know, I studied at the Cathedral School, the seminary of the Archdiocese of New York. Then I wasn't accepted at Fordham, and almost by chance I went to New York University, where, thanks to a professor named Haig Manoogian, I discovered that I could express everything I felt through film.

Could one say that becoming a director represented a way of responding to your faith?

I became a director in order to express my whole self, and also my relationship with religion, which is crucial. And there are those who find in my movies a meditation on a vocation that was never realized or that took other paths. There is no doubt that for me religion is intertwined with, and expressed by, a medium that captivated me the moment my father took me to see *On the Waterfront* and *Rear Window.*

You never finished Jerusalem Jerusalem, *the film in which you tried to express your existential crises more directly.*

It was a very autobiographical story that revolved around a spiritual retreat made by a person called J.R. The treatment recounted in detail processions, sermons, prayers. It originated in my feeling upset about certain teachings.

What are you referring to?

To the problems of an adolescent, such as premarital sex and masturbation, in relation to the teachings of the Church.

In the film that made your name internationally, Mean Streets, *there's a scene in which the protagonist ends the penance given by his confessor by saying: "You don't make up for your sins in church. You do it in the streets."*

I think that repentance and redemption require a constant daily effort. For a believer, the Church has to represent the departure and the point of reference.

A common element of your stories is that no one seems able to escape Golgotha.

I've never thought rationally of a conclusion like that, but I want to answer with a phrase that I noted at the time of *Jerusalem Jerusalem,* and that Bresson used in *Diary of a Country Priest:* "God is not a torturer: he just wants us to have compassion toward ourselves."

What directors whose films have a spiritual dimension do you most admire?

The list would be too long! The first two names that come to mind are Dreyer, in particular for *Ordet* and *Gertrude,* and Frank Borzage, for the way he tells of redemption through love.

Do you admire any directors or works that have no religious dimension at all?

From the way you ask you seem to have an answer in mind.

No, not really. But, for example, I find no spiritual elements in Luchino Visconti, a great director.

I don't agree. Think, for example, of the intimacy of the family ties in *Rocco and His Brothers,* which as you know was inspired by a text drowning in spirituality, Dostoyevsky's *Idiot.* There was a moment when I thought of adapting the novel to the screen, but I stopped when I realized that I would never make a film as beautiful as Visconti's. And think also of *The Leopard,* one of the greatest films of all time. I think there is a profound spirituality in the prince's knowledge of his end. And then that incredible final scene, where the prince prays . . .

It's a prayer to the morning star—almost pagan.

Of course, but the prince prays as he sees a priest and an altar boy going at dawn to bring Communion to someone at home.

In your films violence dominates and at times seems inevitable. Raging Bull *is in fact the story of a man whose unique talent is to do harm.*

But it's also the story of a person who suffers violence at the hands of everyone. Some critics saw in him a Christ figure. I don't want to deny it, but it certainly wasn't a conscious elaboration.

In my opinion, Christological representation is a constant of your films. In The Age of Innocence, *for instance, the element that most fascinates me is the way you describe the character of Ellen Olenska: a woman on whom a world of Pharisees places a crown of thorns.*

She isn't the only one who suffers in that film, but I'd like to answer the way I just did about *Raging Bull*.

Let's switch to a film with an explicit spiritual theme, Kundun. *At the time, some wrote that the way you talk about Buddhism shows the obvious influence of your Catholicism.*

I hope I didn't make mistakes in my representation, but in some ways it would be natural, considering my background and my inner self.

Why, when you directly confronted the figure of Christ, did you decide to remake a novel as controversial as that of Kazantzakis?

There are many films about the Christ of the Gospel. They all respect the orthodox view and some are masterpieces. I was interested in developing to the ultimate a crucial, astonishing concept: the word that is made flesh.

NEW YORK,
JANUARY 2006

DEREK WALCOTT

I Believe That I Believe

When Derek Walcott is in New York he feels a great nostalgia for the swim that he takes every morning in the ocean in front of his house in St. Lucia. "It's something more than a pleasure—it's a real ritual," he explains before he starts talking about the internal rituals around which he has constructed the meaning of his life, "a way of reconnecting every day with something that provides the mysterious sense of eternity." That nostalgia is not confined to waking up to the waters of the Caribbean. He misses the odors, the flavors, and the colors of the world in which he was born, a world that he has celebrated and, after living in the United States for many years, definitively chose. Today he still resides in America for part of the year; he is bound to it by the knowledge of the welcome and the opportunities he has found here. But ever since he has returned to his splendid tropical Ithaca, he has not stopped writing the epic of his land, which is characterized by a slow pace and a pride in mixed origins, as he says in his poems: "I'm just a red nigger who love the sea. / I had a sound colonial education, / I have Dutch, nigger, and English in me, /and either I'm nobody or I'm a nation." He says, "Those are lines from many years ago, but as I get older I realize that truths never change."

What importance does religion have within this particular truth?

A crucial importance: religion is a fact one cannot escape. I've always been sure that it's an illusion to think that one can do without it, or has not been indelibly influenced by it.

A lot of your work immortalizes the melancholy of exile and the anguish that it can bring even to a well-off émigré.

Exile is always painful, but in some ways it's the most classic human condition.

What do you mean?

That the sense of exile experienced by the victim of persecution, by a poor man who flees poverty, or even by someone who simply feels uneasy living where he was born is a metaphor of the exile of the human condition.

From what you say, I assume that you believe in transcendence.

Yes, of course, even though doubts assail my thoughts and my faith.

If I were to ask you explicitly if you believe in God?

I would say I believe that I believe.

And what is this God like?

It's difficult, in fact impossible, to separate it from the image inculcated in me during my childhood.

Which is?

A white man with a beard. Wise and old.

But beyond that image what do you see?

I see only the risk of banality. In some ways, beyond that image doubts begin.

What relationship do you have with this God?

Inconstant.

How can you be inconstant toward an omnipotent being in whom you say you believe?

I said I *believe* that I believe. If I had answered with certainty, my attitude would probably be different. And as for inconstancy, that bears witness to a frailty that no one is exempt from.

But do you pray to this God?

I admit that I almost always pray when I'm in trouble. When I feel stronger and more serene, I express gratitude for life, the most wonderful gift there is.

Was your upbringing religious?

Yes, but with a lay approach. My father was a bohemian artist and my mother a teacher. My relationship with faith was marked by a fundamental fact: I was brought up as a Methodist in an environment that was almost completely Catholic.

What effect did this have?

It accentuated a sense of minority and alienation. For a long time I thought I was living and creating in a blasphemous dimension.

In what sense? What do you mean?

During the period of intellectual formation a choice of minority can strengthen some things and make others rigid. And the contrast, which in itself is always salutary, passes through phases in which certainties are mixed with uncertainties: I recall the feeling of confusion—which has not completely disappeared—roused in me by the difference between the triumphant representation of the divinity of Catholicism and the more austere image of Protestantism.

Once in a lecture you quoted this statement of T. S. Eliot's: "A people's culture is the incarnation of its religion."

Obviously one has to clarify what is meant by religion in a broad sense, but it's absurd to deny the value it carries, which is inescapable and in many cases absolute.

One of the most fascinating interpretations of your work is its celebration of the making of a national identity by glorifying individual stories.

Civilization and culture progress as long as there is harmony between these elements, which in turn are intimately linked to the spiritual.

Jorge Luis Borges wrote, "Men, throughout recorded time, have always told and retold two stories—that of a lost ship which searches the Mediterranean seas for a dearly loved island, and that of a God who is crucified on Golgotha."

As always, it's a remarkable image, and certainly it contains some truth. As you know, the relationship with Homer is fundamental for my culture and for my very existence. Yet as a Christian and as a man who was brought up in a humanistic culture, I have to say that this is true for us

Westerners. But I don't know if one could say the same—at least, with regard to the past—for one born on an island in the Pacific or in Southeast Asia.

For centuries religion was a dominant theme in art. Today it's much rarer to see a religious image.

One could say the same for every art, but this obviously doesn't mean that the religious spirit is lost. There are historical and political reasons, tied to the fact that in the past the Church commissioned a lot of sacred art, and also to the epochal revolutions that have laid the foundations of secularization. But I want to insist that it's not a sudden absence, due perhaps to the discovery, on the part of artists, of a void. I would say, rather, that in these times the meaning and the manifestation of the divinity are to be found in a more indirect approach. It seems to me further that today we are witnessing the phenomenon of a revival of attention paid to religion, a situation that will find greater and greater expression in art.

One of Giorgio de Chirico's most famous paintings is The Nostalgia of the Infinite. *It shows two small human figures in the lower part of a canvas that seems to expand toward immensity.*

It's a metaphor for the human condition, which brings us back to what we were saying about the idea of exile. I think that each of us, leaving aside whatever our convictions may be, feels in his inmost self the sense of something infinitely greater. Faith offers us a key, or rather a way, opposed to mystery, and creates a new one—precisely what believers define as the "mystery of faith."

Your poem "Pentecost" begins with the lines "Better a jungle in the head / than rootless concrete," and concludes with a yearning for "what, in my childhood gospels, / used to be called the Soul."

It's a yearning for the very definition of the soul, not for existence.

What do you mean?

That we live—or at least I feel I live—in a world that has to be confronted first by the intellect. But I think that in the purity of childhood it's easier to perceive, and so imagine, the presence of the soul.

Your cultural education went back and forth between the Caribbean and the United States. What are the main differences that you've found in the approach to religion of these two cultural realities?

This is a huge subject, and when one examines it one tends too often to forget the incredible cultural variousness of the United States. As far as urban America is concerned, the aspect that I would mainly note is the absence of ritual, which in the West Indies is crucial.

Have you ever thought about Rousseau's myth of the noble savage?

Every person who reflects on faith has to think about it.

What's your conclusion?

From a structural point of view, the myth perhaps can't be explored today. Technology makes isolation almost completely impossible. But the truth that the myth conveys remains, and continues to speak to us.

NEW YORK,
MARCH 2003

ELIE WIESEL

I Have a Wounded Faith

Elie Wiesel welcomes me to his study on the Upper East Side on a midwinter day that is unexpectedly springlike. Before starting to talk about his personal relationship with God, he looks for a long time at skyscrapers gilded by the light of sunset. He smiles silently, as if that were already his first response, then he asks me about the political situation in Italy, which he says is "mysterious for anyone who doesn't live there." He has just returned from a long journey through the United States, and is about to leave again for a series of lectures in which he will take up some of the themes we are planning to discuss. "In the end, the existence of God is the only true problem," he says, with a severe expression, "in which all other problems are subsumed and minimized. At times, I think that we are always talking about God without realizing it."

Among the many philosophers who have confronted this subject, Blaise Pascal spoke explicitly of the existence of a hidden God.

Pascal is one of the thinkers I most admire, and he constantly goads me to examine the greatest problems. He wasn't the first to speak of a hidden God. The Bible itself speaks of God who covers his face. And my interpretation—it's not only mine—is that God covers his face because he can't bear what he sees, what we men do.

In his Pensées, *Pascal writes, interpreting God's thought: "You wouldn't seek me if you hadn't already found me."*

It seems to be a phrase that well explains the importance of choice within faith.

Do you believe in God, Professor Wiesel?
Yes, of course.

May I ask what your image of him is?
You can certainly ask, but I have to answer that I don't have an image of him.

Derek Walcott told me that he can't free himself of the image that he was brought up with in childhood: an old, white man with a wise expression.

I understand Walcott's remark, and it's obviously a very human simplification that is hard to get rid of. Yet I think that every image represents a limitation, and that mystery is part of his infinite greatness.

Have you always believed in God?
Since childhood, but I've had my moments of crisis.

And what was the God of your childhood like?
Not very different from the one of adulthood. I can tell you that he was in my dreams, in my prayers, in every aspect of an existence that is otherwise inconceivable.

Were your parents believers?
Yes, they were extremely religious.

How much do you owe your faith to them?
Undoubtedly I owe to my father, Shlomo, and my mother, Sarah, my education and the example they set. But, as happens with everyone, my faith went through a fundamental moment of choice. Otherwise one can't call it faith.

You speak of choice. Some would speak of grace.

I have no problem with defining it like that, provided you don't minimize freedom of choice and the consequences that are assumed the moment you believe.

You studied philosophy at the Sorbonne. Do you think that those studies influenced your faith?

I would say no. Philosophy gave me the terminology, the method, and the ability to articulate in a more rigorous manner my relationship with the problems of existence.

Often in these conversations about faith this phrase of Dostoyevsky's has come up: "If God doesn't exist, everything is permitted."

It's a tragic declaration, which I feel that I share.

How do you conceive existence without faith?

The world has had obvious recent experience of it. The horrors of the century just ended were perpetrated by the godless dictatorship of Nazism and the atheist dictatorship of Communism. This obviously doesn't mean that monstrosities haven't been committed in the name of God; the list of believers who are stained with infamy is long. Yet the programmatic absence of a God, or at least the illusion of opposing his presence, leads systematically to horror.

You believe firmly in God, but you live in a world where suffering, injustice, and tyranny exist.

It's the great torment of my entire existence. The question I don't know how to answer and that I don't think anyone can answer. But even in these terrible moments I see not an absence but, rather, an eclipse.

Do you think that God can permit war?

I think it's more probable that rulers use God and religion to start wars. And I see that this happens constantly, but no one can or will ever be able to demonstrate that a war is fought by the will of God. If it weren't such a tragic subject, one might ask jokingly every time for a notarized statement certifying that the war about to be unleashed has been willed expressly by the Omnipotent.

The politics of our time appeals more and more frequently to prayer.

This is nothing new, just as there is nothing new about the presence of hypocritical, calculating, and often insincere attitudes. It is important to emphasize how enormous the risks can be in the cases mentioned.

Do you pray?

Yes, constantly and simply.

When did you begin?

As a child. But as often happens, my first instinct was emulation: I didn't want to be the last in my family to pray.

And have you always prayed?

No, I've had my moments of crisis, which have led me to study and argue with God, at times dramatically.

How would you define your faith today?

I would use the adjective *wounded,* which I believe may be valid for everyone in my generation. Hasidism teaches that no heart is as whole as a broken heart, and I would say that no faith is as solid as a wounded faith.

Men of faith perceive in prayer the highest moment of spirituality.

Prayer is a fundamental aspect, but I devote a large part of my existence to action: I believe it's a way of interpreting one's own spirituality.

What do you mean?

That there are moments when it's necessary to interfere with what happens in history. For example, when life and human dignity are in danger, different cultures become irrelevant. The moment a person is persecuted for his race, his religion, his political ideas, he becomes—for those who think they have a religious spirit—the center of the universe.

Another writer who has been cited in this meditation on religion is Isaac Bashevis Singer, whose novel The Family Moskat *ends with the words "Death is the Messiah. That's the real truth."*

I knew Singer well, and I think it's right to place him among the writers who investigated this sort of problem very effectively. But it's impossible to take the ending of *The Family Moskat* out of context: it's a conclusion for an effect, and it coincides with the rise of Nazism and the end not only of a family but of an entire cultural and religious experience.

You don't think that that is the greatest wound?

Of course, but to sanctify death seems to deny faith. And there I do not go. In fact I believe the contrary.

Can you name an artist you admire who openly professes a faith different from yours?

I have the greatest respect for anyone who has a faith, whatever it is. Even for those who are atheists and believe firmly in the nonexistence of God.

Can I assume that you are opposed to every kind of fundamentalism?

Absolutely. Fanaticism is a danger, whether it's the Muslims, the Christians, or the Jews. And respect for the faith of others, which I truly believe in, requires equal respect on the part of the other. When I am thinking of my personal experience, there comes to mind, as a luminous example, François Mauriac. I, a Jew, owe to the fervent Catholic Mauriac, who declared himself in love with Christ, the fact of having become a writer.

Do you think that the God Mauriac believed in is different from the one you believe in?

No. But I know how different our views can be, and our approach. Once Mauriac dedicated a book to me and he wrote: "To Elie Wiesel, a Jewish child who was crucified." At first I took it badly, but then I understood that it was his way of letting me feel his love.

NEW YORK,
FEBRUARY 2003

ACKNOWLEDGMENTS

This book has a biblical beginning: it was born from the rib of a survey conducted in 2003 for *La Repubblica*. I want to thank Paolo Mauri, who allowed me to publish it in the culture pages, and also the editor, Ezio Mauro. Both had a confidence in me for which I can never be grateful enough.

My warmest thanks go also to Vincenzo Ostuni, a passionate and frank editor even in the (few) moments of disagreement; to the indefatigable and patient Ornella Mastrobuoni; to the ironic and stubborn Martina Donati; and to Elido Fazi, with whom I am pleased to have undertaken this second journey. I would like to thank Sarah Chalfant, whose intelligence, generosity, and friendship have immeasurably enriched me; LuAnn Walther, who believed in this book and its author; and Ann Goldstein, for her patience, elegance, and dedication.

Some of the interviews in this book were made possible thanks to the invaluable help of some friends: I am grateful to Gianni Ferrari, Carla Tanzi, Nicole Aragi, Marianne Merola, Meg Giles, and Emma Tillinger. Finally I want to thank all those who were interviewed for their patience and their willingness to speak about private subjects, and I say farewell sadly to Grace Paley, Arthur Schlesinger, Jr., and to the great Saul Bellow. The faith that joins us through our different rituals tells me that we will meet again.

I wish to conclude by expressing as always my gratitude to my brother Andrea for his many suggestions and his unconditional affection. It was he who brought to my attention the wonderful quotation from Borges that I cited at the beginning of the book.